Professional development in school

Joan Dean

Open University Press
Milton Keynes · Philadelphia

Open University Press
Celtic Court
22 Ballmoor
Buckingham
MK18 1XW

and
1900 Frost Road, Suite 101
Bristol, PA 19007, USA

First Published 1991

British Library Cataloguing in Publication Data

Dean, Joan
    Professional development in School.—(England Teachers and teaching)
    1. England. Teachers. In-service training
    I. Title   II. Series
    371.1460942

    ISBN 0-335-09591-7 (hb)
    ISBN 0-335-09590-9 (pb)

Library of Congress Cataloging-in-Publication Data

Dean, Joan.
    Professional development in school / Joan Dean.
      p. cm.—(Developing teachers and teaching series)
    Includes bibliographical references and index.
    ISBN 0-335-09591-7—ISBN 0-335-09590-9 (pbk.)
    1. Teachers—In-service training—Great Britain. 2. Career
development—Great Britain. 3. Teachers—Great Britain—Rating of.
I. Title. II. Series.
LB1731.D43 1991
371.1'46—dc20   90-45382
                                                    CIP

Typeset by Rowland Phototypesetting Ltd
Bury St Edmunds, Suffolk
Printed in Great Britain by Biddles Ltd
Guildford and King's Lynn

To my friends in the Surrey Inspectorate

Contents

List of figures

Series editor's introduction

The 1980s saw a host of legislated reforms in teachers' conditions of service, the curriculum, and the governance and accountabilities of schools and LEAs. These reforms took place within the context of falling school rolls, and an ageing and increasingly static and embattled teaching profession. Thus the 1990s hold a particular challenge for those responsible for the management of professional development.

The 1990s will witness the continuing implementation of the changes initiated in the 1980s. This process will have to be managed with commitment and skill by all teachers, but a particular responsibility will continue to fall upon headteachers and other senior staff to ensure that teachers' learning needs are taken into account explicitly within the context of what at the time of writing appear to be increasingly prescriptive models of curriculum content and assessment, systems of teacher appraisal, and performance indicators for schools.

In this book, Joan Dean, herself an experienced practitioner at primary and secondary levels and formerly Chief Schools Inspector for Surrey, provides in her writing the kind of practical understanding and support which are appropriate to all those in 'locally managed' schools who are faced with the responsibilities and challenges of maintaining staff morale, minimizing stress levels while providing appropriate challenge and support, and building programmes of professional and institutional appraisal and development which take account of adult learning needs. The author discusses personal and social dimensions of professional development and the skills and knowledge needed by all teachers in primary, secondary and special schools from induction onwards. In every chapter she provides detailed practical guidelines for promoting professional development within a positive school culture, focusing particularly upon planning for processes of needs identification, school review, design of in-service events, teacher records, school evaluation, teacher appraisal, and the role of management in professional development.

At the heart of the book is Joan Dean's concern, first and foremost, with the learning needs of the young person at school. Her broad experience enables her to draw upon a range of authoritative sources so that the mosaic which she constructs avoids the dangers of parochialism and single voice narrative. Her book thus provides opportunities for all who are serious about professional development to reflect upon its purposes, processes and outcomes and to plan sensitively, practically and intelligently for the continuing committed and skilled support of teachers and teaching in the 1990s.

Christopher Day

Preface

Changes in the responsibilities of LEAs and schools are resulting in a much greater responsibility for professional development for the schools. The former situation in which the LEA and others provided a programme of courses from which teachers selected those which interested them is giving way to a different pattern in which the school is responsible for the professional development of its staff and must decide and to some extent provide what is necessary, drawing on other providers to contribute to its own programme.

This book is intended to help schools – primary, secondary and special – to plan and implement their professional development programme. After a general introduction it looks at the way teachers learn and at the range of learning opportunities available in the course of normal school work. It goes on to consider the professional development policy, needs assessment and the building of a programme. There is a detailed account of how to plan and carry out an in-service event, with information about the possible ways of enabling adults to learn. A substantial section deals with appraisal and looks at the work which must be done in looking at the different aspects of a teacher's performance prior to the appraisal interview. The interview is dealt with in some detail and there is a short section on providing records, with a number of examples in the appendices. The contribution of other providers is considered in the relation to the school programme and the advantages of each are considered. The book ends with a chapter on evaluation which gives a good deal of information about different ways of undertaking this.

What is professional development?

Professional development and change

We are currently in the midst of unprecedented change in education. Almost everything is apparently changing and the rate of change is accelerating. The role of the LEA, school governors, headteachers and teachers will all be different in the future from what they have been in the past and everything is happening at a very fast rate, which leaves us little time to become acclimatized to new ways of looking at things.

In addition to change coming at us from government, we also have the changes resulting from the rapid development of knowledge which is making existing knowledge out-of-date very quickly. A great deal that we are currently teaching in schools, if not already out of date, will become so in the very near future.

The speed of change and the explosion of knowledge are requiring people to learn afresh at intervals throughout their lives. This has important implications for the role of the school, which is no longer that of providing a package of knowledge and skills to serve a person for life. Now that it is possible to have vast stores of knowledge available at the touch of a key, the emphasis in initial schooling needs to be on the process of learning. Today's children and young people need a level of knowledge which enables them to fit new learning into a coherent framework but above all they need to know how to sort out information so that they can apply it in new situations. This places an emphasis on the skills of independent learning and on learning how to learn including the application of what is learned. Most of the developments we have seen recently, such as GCSE and TVEI, have reflected this.

There is another sense in which new technology is affecting schools. The computer can teach some things more easily than a teacher because if programmed properly it can provide a one-to-one match for the stage the pupil is at and can modify the programme according to the pupil's answers. This is not yet happening because we are still at an early stage of exploring the possibilities that information technology offers us, but it will come.

Computers are also available to many children and young people at home; parents will not be slow to buy software which can help their children's learning. As the range of computers and software expands and becomes cheaper this will have a tremendous effect on schools. Schools will eventually reach the point where a great deal of the skill learning is done with the aid of the computer and could actually be done at home. Already there is news of some American schools giving students computers to use at home and thus making the need to be in school all the time unnecessary. This has important implications for the role of the teacher. It leaves the teacher to do the things that a human being does better than a computer, such as being sensitive to pupil's needs, planning for them and with them, using the computer and other materials. The teacher has an important role in selecting and helping children and young people to use and respond to first-hand experiences, in making them aware of the environment and of other people, in helping them to become independent learners.

Children and young people also need to learn socially and experience group activities. They need to know how to work with other people to agreed ends; they need the experience of activities such as drama and music-making and games which need a group.

Another source of change, particularly in the primary school, is the effect of the studies of child development and children's learning. These have shown us many things, such as the effects of home environment on the ability to learn at school; the stages of children's development and the implications of these for the curriculum at each stage; what actually happens in classrooms as distinct from what appears to be happening; the relationship between teaching style and pupils' achievement; the effects of different kinds of organization and teaching methods and much else. This knowledge has been developing over a long period and is gradually affecting what is done not only at the primary but also now at the secondary stage.

Jacquetta Megarry[1] points out that

> Teachers must develop and capitalize on those skills which are not easily replaced by microelectronic devices – human and personal skills of communication, motivation and counselling, design skills for producing computer based software and evaluation and research skills to assess the impact of the media and methods. These are different from the skills currently possessed and valued by the teaching profession, and they may be distributed differently among the population from which it draws.

Education in the future will demand a highly skilled teaching profession but of a different character and perhaps reduced in size.

There is currently a much greater concern with the professional development of teachers than existed ten years ago. This is not only that the demands of the National Curriculum and all that has come with the Education Reform Act 1988[2] is forcing change upon us. We have become conscious that children and young people have a greater potential than we have been able to tap in schools hitherto. There is stress on accountability. There is the pressure of competition for pupils and also competition for promotion. We have also become dissatisfied with some of the models of development which were current formerly because we know a lot more than we once did about the way adults learn. Many things have come together to place a greater emphasis on the need for teachers to develop and learn.

Financial stringency in the education service over a long period has increased society's concern with teacher performance as well as development. In the past it was often possible for a school to carry its less effective brethren; many LEAs were sympathetic to the problem of the school which had a weak teacher and were a bit more generous over staffing. This has become less possible in recent years; in future with governors of schools carrying the responsibility for their staffing it is unlikely that such teachers will survive.

Most of the changes taking place have possibilities. They could help to create better schools and better learning opportunities for children and young people. The extent to which they are successful depends upon a number of people, but on none more than headteachers and teachers. If we are to manage change rather than be managed by it, we need to see that as far as possible the staffs of schools are able to cope with what is happening. This is something which must come from within the schools, although those outside can do much to support headteachers and teachers in dealing with the changes affecting them.

Accountability and the need for professional development

A major way in which education has changed in the last few years is in the greater emphasis on accountability. This emphasis is likely to increase with the Education Reform Act 1988, which is placing the responsibility for education much more clearly with the school and its headteachers and governors and emphasizing also the idea of competition between schools.

Schools therefore need to be concerned about their clients. These involve various groups of people. John Wilson[3] suggests that HMI might be regarded as a representative client from the educational world and we might add to HMI the local authority inspectorate, who will have an increasing role in assessing what schools are doing. John Pearce[4] notes that HMI use six sets of criteria in judging what is happening in a school – plant, match, pedagogy, progression,

Inspection

professionalism and climate. HMI reports have been published since 1981 and there are a number of areas common to many reports in which they find schools deficient. These have important implications for professional development. They find that there are generally a lack of departmental policies and statements of curriculum which link with school statements of aims and policies. Curriculum generally lacks progression and coherence and there is insufficient differentiation to cater for the full range of ability, particularly the most able who are under-extended.

These findings might be linked with the findings of the study by Valerie Hall, Hugh Mackay and Colin Morgan,[5] which found many of the professional tasks of leadership not undertaken by headteachers, particularly those of professional development. When this finding is linked with the finding of the HMI paper *Ten Good Schools*,[6] which stresses the importance of the headteacher in determining the quality of the school, it suggests that there is a substantial learning task for headteachers themselves as well as in developing other teachers.

pupils

Pupils might be expected to have a view as clients of the school: there is a sense in which teachers are accountable to them. Pupils expect to be well taught by teachers who have prepared their work. They respect teachers who make demands upon them, care about them as individuals, are fair, mark work carefully and take homework seriously.

parents

Parents also expect these things on behalf of their children. In addition, they expect to be treated as partners in many respects in that they expect to be informed about what is happening and consulted. It is perhaps worth noting that teachers are not trained in working with parents but the demands of the Education Reform Act 1988 require a much greater level of consultation as it will be necessary to talk with parents about each pupil's progress through the testing system. Every school will need to place some emphasis on the skills of doing this as part of its professional development programme.

Another group of clients are employers who are asking for greater emphasis on the skills which may be required for working life. As a nation we appear to have done less well than some others in preparing our young people for work, partly because we have always stressed the importance of initial education being broad and general and have felt that vocational schemes were limiting. If the schemes which have a vocational content are narrowly based this is no doubt true, but if we take the view that process is important, many skills and kinds of understanding can be developed as well through vocational courses as non-vocational and for many young people, the vocational courses provide a motivation which may be lacking in some other work.

Teacher development

The terms 'staff development', 'professional development' and 'in-service education' tend to be used interchangeably for both the process of individual development and that of organizational growth. For example Graham Williams[7] suggests that staff development

> is the process by which individuals, groups and organisations learn to be more effective and efficient.

Cawood and Gibbon[8] describe staff development as

> an experiential involvement by a teacher in the process of growing. This process is not short term. It is a continuous, never ending developmental activity.

Roland Morant[9] says (of in-service education):

> It is the education intended to support and assists the professional development that teachers ought to experience through their working lives.

These definitions do not differentiate among the terms in-service education, staff development and professional development.

The term 'professional development' suggests a process whereby teachers become more professional. The term 'profession' implies a number of things. The most commonly accepted definitions of a profession are of an occupation which requires a long training, involves theory as a background to practice, has its own code of behaviour and has a high degree of autonomy. All of these apply to teachers. A further definition of a profession is a group which is in charge of the admission of its own new members. This clearly does not.

If one follows the first group of definitions above one might see someone who is professional as having a substantial background of knowledge and skill, acquired during initial training and thereafter. One would expect a professional person to be highly ethical within the terms of that profession. He or she might also be expected to be highly committed and able to stand back from current situations and see them in perspective. Professional teachers would also be expected to work together for the good of the school or college. Professional development can therefore be seen as an increase in some aspect of professionalism and can legitimately be applied to the development of individuals or of groups if the purpose of the activity is the increase of professionalism.

School-focused professional development

The whole process of professional development has changed radically in recent years. One landmark of change was DES Circular 6/86,[10] which had as a main purpose

> to promote more systematic and purposeful planning of in-service training.

The Circular was also concerned

> to promote the professional development of teachers; to encourage more effective management of the teaching force and to encourage training in selected areas which are to be accorded priority.

Although in-service education has been in being for a long time, we know remarkably little about its effect. William Taylor[11] points out that we know little about the type of experience likely to create professional growth, the relationship of such growth to student learning and the effect of different kinds of professional development on individual careers.

The major change in emphasis in in-service work is from courses provided by those outside the school to professional development as a school-focused activity. School-focused in-service work was described by Pauline Perry[12] at an OECD/CERI International Workshop as

> all the strategies employed by trainers and teachers in partnership to direct teaching programmes in such a way as to meet the identified needs of a school and to raise the standards of teaching and learning in the classroom.

Roland Morant[9] suggested that school-focused in-service education should have the following features:

1 It would serve the school's institutional needs and, therefore, educational needs.
2 It would be intended for teachers actually serving at the school.
3 It would be initiated and planned by members of the school staff.
4 It would be led and executed by members of the school staff.
5 It would utilize the school's physical resources.
6 It would take place on school premises.

This is a very strict definition. National moves in in-service education have required LEAs to ask their schools for staff development plans and the move to give responsibility for spending to schools and their governors has placed them in a quite different position from that which obtained in 1981 when the statement above was written. Schools are now in a position to buy at least some of what they need and are likely to use a variety of sources to help them with the programme they plan. They may also decide to meet outside the school premises and use resources provided by the LEA or a higher education institution or a hotel.

The definition above does not mention the need for the professional development programme being in accord with the school aims and philosophy. This is important since the programme of professional development, whatever the needs of individuals, is also a programme for developing the school. This can happen only if it reinforces the school's aims.

School-focused in-service education has been around for a long time but the difference between the past and present is that now the school is truly responsible and will have money to carry out its responsibility. This makes it possible to match the needs of individual teachers much more closely than has been the case formerly. This demands careful work on the part of the school both to analyse the needs of the staff and to provide for them. The individual teacher is most likely to develop professionally when the school is supportive and the school is most likely to develop in a local and national climate which is supportive. Mutual support is an essential element in the development process.

mutual support

The professional development programme

Bruce Joyce[13] suggests that a comprehensive programme of professional development should fulfil three functions. It should

1 provide adequate systems of in-service training for all teachers
2 provide support for schools that will enable them to fulfil their programmes
3 create a context in which teachers are enabled to develop their potential.

He suggests that there are three needs for professional development to fulfil:

1 the social need for an efficient and humane educational system capable of adaptation to evolving social needs
2 the need to find ways of helping educational staff to improve the wider personal, social and academic potential of the young people in the neighbourhood
3 the need to develop and encourage the teacher's desire to live a satisfying and stimulating personal life, which by example as well as by precept will help his students to develop and fulfil each his own potential.

Thus professional development is seen as offering something to society, to the pupils and to the teacher.

Professional development is career long, starting with initial training and continuing until retirement. It is an active process. The teacher must actually work to develop. Development does not happen merely as a result of years of teaching. Tom Peters, an American business trainer, in a seminar in London, spoke of a firm where there was a daily meeting at which staff were each asked what developments they had made in their work since the previous meeting. While the daily request would seem to be a somewhat over-frequent use of this question, it nevertheless stresses the need for development to be a continual day-to-day process for staff and a regular responsibility for management to encourage it. People in senior posts in schools might well ask this question more frequently than they do at present.

The statement of school-focused work given earlier stressed the need for teachers to be involved in the planning and execution of the programme. The present situation not only makes it possible for schools to look more widely for contributors to their programme, but also relies upon them to seek out skills and abilities among the staff and use them as far as possible. This may mean training teachers and others who work in the schools in the skills of presenting materials to adults.

The learning context

We have already noted that the school in which a teacher works has a strong and lasting influence on that teacher's development. This is a matter not only of the overt behaviour of the headteacher and staff of the school, but also of the entire school culture. The values adopted by the headteacher and staff and the attitudes current in the staffroom are crucial to the development of those who work there. A school where the headteacher and senior staff work to ensure that attitudes are positive, where children and young people matter, where there is a feeling that problems are there to be solved, not only is more likely to be offering its pupils a good education but also is likely to be developing its staff.

Anyone concerned with professional development, whether within the school or outside it, must take into account the school culture if any work done with the staff is to have effect. Assessment of needs requires an assessment of attitudes if it is to be of value in guiding the school towards a programme which will be effective.

The TRIST Guidelines to LEAs[14] suggested that successful in-service education should

1 have clear objectives
2 be based on careful identification of teachers' needs and institutional needs
3 start from teachers' current levels of knowledge and skills
4 be carefully monitored and evaluated
5 be clearly costed and ensure value for money
6 have the support of the head/principal for follow-up practice after training
7 be part of a continuing process of professional development.

Three further points might be made about professional development. It is, above all, about improving the experience for pupils in the classroom. Unless it does this, it is an extravagance which we should not be prepared to afford. Second, it should benefit the staff. Third, it should concern everyone in the school, from the head to the ancillary staff. It is not simply a matter for teachers at certain stages of their careers.

2

Teachers learning

The school as a learning place for teachers

Michael Eraut[15] makes the point that we can only foster the natural process of teacher development, but that the rate and direction of development depend upon three things:

1 the knowledge, experience and personality of the teacher
2 the school context; and
3 professional contact and discussion outside the school.

We saw in Chapter 1 that the school a teacher works in affects his or her development. We can put this more positively and say that the school is the major learning place for teachers as well as children. We also need to consider the way in which the development of the school and the development of teachers interact.

McCormick and James[16] state that 'effective change depends upon the genuine commitment of those required to implement it'. They suggest that

> commitment can only be achieved if those involved feel they have control of the process. . . . Teachers will readily seek to improve their performance if they regard it as part of their professional accountability, whereas they will resist change that is forced upon them.

This poses considerable problems for those responsible for professional development, since a good deal of the present change is coming from outside the school. Headteachers and LEA staff have an important role in helping teachers generally to come to terms with these changes and make them their own.

Teachers are more likely to feel in control of the process if they see their own development as part of the development of their school. School development goes hand in hand with the professional development of teachers. The teachers need to develop in order for the school to develop. Without school development, it is difficult, though not impossible, for individual teachers to develop.

Professional development in school can be seen from the point of view of the aims of the particular school or the needs of the individual.

The everyday life of the school is the major source of learning for teachers. There is a sense in which everything that happens in a school has possibilities for their learning. Each new group of pupils brings new problems and challenges. Each change in the way the school functions provides opportunities for learning new ways of doing things; every task to be done has learning possibilities for someone; every problem requires new thinking.

Of course it is not possible to use every opportunity. Often the need is to get the job done or the problem solved quickly. Yet the opportunities are always there and the learning possibilities are infinite. Their use is partly a matter of an attitude of mind on the part of the management of the school and the individual teachers within it.

A teacher entering the teaching profession newly qualified brings a body of knowledge from training and the beginnings of the skills needed by a teacher. The school in which a teacher starts his or her career is probably the most important single source of learning for that teacher from then on; it is likely to affect the way he or she works for many years, perhaps throughout teaching life. This is so whether or not the headteacher and staff make a conscious effort to help the teacher to develop. Newly qualified teachers are impressionable at the beginning of their careers and the examples they are shown are important. It is in the context of actually doing the job that each teacher practises and develops teaching skills and acquires and consolidates knowledge.

Michael Eraut[15] also makes the point that just as the expectation of the teacher raises the level of performance of the pupil, so the expectation of teachers demonstrated by the headteacher and senior management of the school affects their performance.

Teachers learn through interaction with their professional environment. In this context, the treatment a new teacher receives from those in senior posts, the extent to which his or her views are considered and treated with respect, the expectations demonstrated and the attitudes shown all contribute to the teacher's development. New teachers form and develop a frame of reference by which they judge their own professional activity and that of others. They acquire new knowledge and develop the skills to meet the tasks and the situations they encounter. The school can therefore be a very important place of learning for the teacher.

What do teachers need to learn?

Before we can consider how teachers can develop their work, we need to consider the kind of development which is desirable. There would seem to be three main areas in which teachers may develop:

1 They need to acquire appropriate background knowledge.
2 They can develop their classroom teaching skills, including the skills involved in the pastoral care of pupils and the administrative tasks of the classroom.
3 Some teachers will have a management role within the school and this too is an area for development.

Background knowledge

Terms and conditions of employment

All teachers need to know about the working of the profession, the terms and conditions of employment and the law as it affects them.

School information

Teachers need detailed information about their own jobs, where they fit into the school and what is required from them. They need to know the school philosophy and policies; patterns of responsibility and communication channels; organization and pastoral care patterns; routines; patterns of assessment for pupils; overall assessment patterns; ways in which their work may be assessed; normal contacts with parents and with other institutions and bodies; information about individual pupils which is relevant for teaching and pastoral care; LEA practice and available support for them.

Child development

Teachers need knowledge of the way children and young people normally develop and learn if they are to understand those they teach and recognize deviations from the norm. They need to know the normal patterns of physical, intellectual, emotional and social development.

Theoretical knowledge of learning

Teachers are more effective when they have adequate theoretical backing for what they do and can use their theoretical knowledge to improve their practice. They need knowledge of theories of learning and teaching and skill in applying them.

Classroom practice

At the beginning of a teaching career, a teacher needs to develop as a person in relation to pupils. The teacher's personality and personal qualities are crucial factors in success. Most children learn better when they like and respect their teacher; a teacher who is a rounded and mature human being offers a model to young people which may affect their attitudes to school, to learning and the world at large in important ways.

Classroom teaching skill will vary according to the teaching task in hand but there are some elements which are common to most good teaching. They are discussed in detail here.

The motivation of pupils

The good teacher is a skilled motivator. This may be because the teacher is an enthusiast for the material being learned or it may be that he or she is particularly sensitive to the pupils, recognizing what motivates them and relating this knowledge to the material they are being asked to learn. It is also a matter of using this sensitivity to decide how to present material to be learned so that it is motivating in its own right.

Content knowledge

A teacher must have mastery of teaching material if he or she is to be truly effective. This does not mean knowing all the answers. There are some situations in which teacher and children can find out together. The teacher must know how to make such a search, however.

Communication skills

A teacher needs communication skills of a high order. These involve not only skill in exposition but also skill in leading discussion, questioning, eliciting responses from individuals, ability to explain, to select appropriate material and help pupils to see what is significant in what is under consideration.

Ability to observe children and young people

A teacher needs skill in observing pupils in the classroom in order to recognize each pupil's needs and progress. An extension of this skill is the ability to use tests and other assessment procedures and to maintain appropriate records.

Skill in recognizing the stage the pupil has reached

Learning takes place most easily if the teacher is aware of the experience each pupil brings to the learning process. This is extremely difficult to do in large classes and impossible if all children are expected to do the same work. Good teaching therefore involves both skill in assessing the stages pupils have reached and then organizing to meet their varying needs.

The ability to plan and organize

Organizing and planning skills are very important to a teacher. They involve not only the ability to plan a programme of work for a given group, but also the ability to create a learning atmosphere and environment, select appropriate teaching methods, identify and solve problems in the classroom, help pupils to become independent and plan ahead.

The ability to help pupils to structure their learning

What a pupil learns remains only if it is related to an appropriate mental structure. The process of making structures in the mind comes naturally to some pupils and not to others. The effective teacher leads pupils to make structures, not actually making the structures but skilled at helping others to make them.

The ability to help pupils develop cognitive skills

The good teacher teaches pupils how to learn through the process of structuring learning and the development of skills such as classifying and ordering, sorting and organizing knowledge and applying it in new situations.

The ability to coach pupils in skills

This is more relevant in practical than academic subjects but coaching skill may be needed in matters such as essay writing or mathematical tasks.

Skill in problem-solving

Teaching is often a problem-solving activity and the good teacher must be a good problem solver as well as a good teacher of problem-solving.

Skill in controlling children and young people

Appropriate learning will take place only if the teacher is in control of the situation. This is partly linked to the skill of organizing so that different abilities are catered for, but is also a matter of the way the teacher treats pupils and the relationships which he or she is able to form with them.

Teaching in school depends upon the ability of teachers to manage children in groups. The skill with which an experienced teacher manages groups of children normally reflects an understanding of the way groups work, even if this is not really conscious. Knowledge of the way groups control individuals and an ability to recognize the effect of both competition and co-operation are valuable to all teachers.

Evaluative skills

As the teacher develops skills he or she gradually acquires internalized standards appropriately related to the pupils involved, knowledge of methods of evaluating, skill in observing progress and in assessing the processes by which the ends were attained.

Management skills and knowledge

A teacher progressing to a more senior level will need not only the skills of the classroom teacher but also various management skills, which are described here.

The ability to articulate and implement aims and policies

Those in management roles need to be able to lead their colleagues in thinking about the aims of the school and how to turn them into action.

The articulation of the curriculum philosophy

They also need to lead thinking about curriculum, including continuity and progression, so that coherence is ensured for the individual pupil.

The management of care and discipline

Management involves creating structures and systems for care and discipline and seeing that these are implemented.

The management of people

Managers need to deal with people not only within the school, but also outside it, such as parents, governors, LEA, etc. They need skill in eliciting ideas from colleagues and drawing them together; such skills as counselling, discussion leadership, presentation skills, negotiating skills, communication and so on. Management also involves staff selection, development, deployment and appraisal.

The management of resources

There will be increasing amounts of work involved in managing the resources of the school as the Education Reform Act 1988 comes into being. Managing resources involves managing the school office and looking after the school building.

Evaluation

Evaluation is an important part of the work of management, whether this be evaluation of the work of individuals or of the school as a whole. Much evaluation should be a joint activity with all the staff taking part, but it needs to be led by management.

All teachers should try to maintain a range of interests outside education and spend some of their time with people who are not in the education business. They also need time for personal refreshment.

Management responsibility for teacher development

If teachers are to acquire and maintain all the abilities listed above, they need to go on adding to their subject knowledge and developing the skills of motivating different generations of children and young people who change in their reactions as the years go by. Skill in recognizing the stage pupils have reached needs continuing development as subject matter changes. A school also needs to prepare teachers for management roles as they become more experienced.

It is the responsibility of the management of a school to see that

1 There is a school policy for staff development, which should help the school to fulfil its aims and is concerned with the development of all staff.
2 There is a staff development programme which includes everyone.
3 There is planned development for all.

Teacher motivation

The process of professional development is concerned with change in teacher activity. This needs to be backed by changes in attitudes and thinking and is consequently a very complex process. Michael Fullan[17] suggests that the implications for the individual teacher involved in change are as follows:

1 Change takes place over time.
2 The initial stages of any substantial change always involve anxiety and uncertainty.
3 Ongoing technical and psychological support assistance is crucial if the anxiety is to be coped with.
4 Change involves learning new skills through practice and feedback; it is incremental and developmental.

5 The most fundamental breakthrough occurs when people can cognitively understand the underlying conception and rationale with respect to why this new way works better.

6 Organizational conditions within the school (peer norms, administrative leadership) and in relation to the school (e.g. external administrative support and technical help) make it more or less likely that the process will succeed.

7 Successful change involves pressure, but it is pressure through interaction with peers and other technical and administrative leaders.

Teacher motivation is an important part of teacher development. We need to consider how teachers are motivated, what they need to learn and how development takes place.

Teachers vary in what motivates them and any individual school planning staff development must take this into account. Motivation will probably operate differently at different periods of a person's career and men and women tend to differ in some aspects of what motivates them. Not all the motivating forces can be used by the school at any given time because they may be outside its control (promotion opportunities, for example) but knowledge of them is still valuable in helping individuals and in thinking out how to provide a programme which will be effective for as many people as possible.

What motivates teachers?

Teachers may be motivated by a number of factors.

Children and young people developing and learning

Most teachers gain satisfaction from seeing that a pupil has learned something new or has acquired a skill as a result of the teacher's efforts. Over a longer period there is satisfaction in seeing a pupil develop and mature. Most teachers are prepared to learn afresh themselves in order to gain this kind of job satisfaction.

Enthusiasm for subject matter

Learning is often caught as much as taught. A teacher who really cares about his/her subject matter will want to maintain skill and knowledge at a high level. Enthusiasm may also make a teacher ready to work at improving teaching skill in order to share a love of the subject with pupils.

Recognition, interest, praise and encouragement

Teachers are as susceptible as anyone else to praise and encouragement and recognition of the work they do. It is the task of management to see that sufficient recognition and praise is offered.

A chance to contribute and to shine

Human beings normally want to contribute to the group in which they find themselves and to gain recognition for this. Most people are also motivated by the opportunity to show others how well they can do. It is a task for the management of a school to see that all teachers get appropriate opportunities to contribute and gain recognition.

A chance to take responsibility

Many people will rise to demands they feel are important. Opportunities to take responsibility are highly motivating to some people and should be widely distributed.

A challenge to professional skill

The exercise of skill is very satisfying. Many teachers rise to the challenge posed by a difficult pupil or class or a request to work at some new task.

The inspiration of others

Individual teachers within a school and others outside may have the ability to inspire their colleagues through their own excitement over something.

Career prospects

Many teachers, particularly the younger ones, are motivated by the prospect of promotion but it is important not to let this take precedence over other forms of motivation because it cannot operate for the whole of a teacher's career. Teachers who have reached the peak of their career may need to find other motivation, especially if they were promoted to their present posts at a comparatively young age and have little prospect of going further.

School policy, status and motivators

David Trethowan[18] gives his own variation of the 'hygiene factors' found by Herzberg,[19] who identified a number of aspects of an organization which must be right before people can think positively about the way forward. Trethowan lists some items which are part of school policy, some items which he calls status, which are to do with the overall conditions of service of the job, and he also gives a list of positive motivators.

School policy

1 school image
2 quality of administration

3 relationships with management
4 supervision by management
5 other affecting relationships, e.g. pupils, parents, colleagues.

Status

1 job security
2 working conditions
3 salary
4 fringe benefits
5 conditions of service, e.g. supervisory duties.

Positive motivators

1 achievements
2 recognition by management
3 the job itself
4 delegated responsibility
5 advancement
6 personal growth
7 cash, particularly related to a specific achievement.

All these motivators can be used by the headteacher and senior management of the school. It can be particularly helpful when considering how to deal with a teacher who appears to be apathetic, to consider which of the possible motivators might be effective. Most of them are, in effect, the same techniques as are used to motivate children and young people.

Initial and in-service training

Initial training

Teachers are often critical of what happens in initial training, failing to realize that there is no way in which students in three or four years can learn everything they need to know as teachers and, at the same time, increase their knowledge in given subject areas. Initial training is only the beginning of learning to be a teacher.

There are, nevertheless, certain aspects of learning which are important in initial training. It is here that the foundation of theory for teaching must be laid. If teachers do not start to acquire the theoretical knowledge which should back their teaching during their initial training, some will write off theory as irrelevant. The ability to relate theory and practice needs to be part of the initial training process so that it becomes second nature. Teachers in initial training need to learn about child development, the way children and young people learn and group management techniques. They also need to acquire a problem-solving attitude to teaching, one in which each new task is a problem which can be tackled and solved.

How do teachers learn?

Joyce and Showers,[20] writing on the ecology of teacher development, give the following components of teaching (of teachers):

1 presentation of theory
2 modelling or demonstration of skills or models
3 practice in simulated or classroom settings
4 structured feedback
5 open-ended feedback
6 coaching for application.

This is a valid description of the way in which teachers in initial training learn much of their professional knowledge and skill. At later stages teacher learning is actually a much more haphazard affair. A teacher encounters a particular problem in the classroom and is stimulated to try out a new idea to meet it. Two teachers compare notes about the way they are doing something and learn as a result. Something is said at a staff meeting which for one teacher pulls together thoughts which have been in his or her mind for a long time. A teacher is asked to undertake a particular piece of work and learns as a result. This haphazard kind of learning is fairly typical of much human learning and although it cannot be controlled the opportunities it presents can be sought out and used. It does not invalidate the need for more formal learning but it must be taken into account as an important part of teacher learning. It is easy to assume that the only learning which takes place is formal learning. We often make the same mistake with children and young people.

Joyce and Showers[20] also stress the need for coaching as part of the learning process. This happens in initial training but is rare in in-service training; we perhaps need to give more thought to ways in which this could be offered as part of teacher learning.

The professional development programme should include all those areas identified above.

Professional development is first of all a matter of the personal development which enables a person to tackle new tasks, relate well to others, see important issues and so on. Part of this development is the acquisition of specific skills, knowledge and understanding, both for the classroom and for management. This knowledge, skill and understanding gradually needs to become internalized and refined so that it becomes part of the teacher's professional personality and is available when needed.

There are some important differences in teaching adults as compared with children. Children, particularly young children, have not yet formed thinking structures in many areas and part of the teacher's work is to help them to form such structures. Adults have formed structures in many areas of thinking and their perception is also coloured by the attitudes and views they have acquired. On the one hand this makes learning easier because new learning fits into an existing structure. On the other hand it can be an impediment to new thinking because it is difficult to think outside existing structures and attitudes.

Honey and Mumford[21] suggest that there are four preferred learning styles: activitist, reflector, theorist and pragmatist. Another typology suggests four slightly different styles:

1 Assimilator – assimilates new learning into existing structures.
2 Shaper – creates new structures to accommodate new learning.
3 Detail learner – concentrates on the detail rather than the overall pattern.
4 Passive learner – takes learning as it comes, sometimes concentrating on detail and sometimes assimilating to existing structures.

It would seem likely that the shaper among this group will be the person who takes in most of what is being offered. Teachers need help in structuring their learning and this is important in planning work with them. Opportunities to group, order and classify material are important.

It is also important to consider ways in which the bridge can be made between what happens in the in-service course and what happens in the classroom. Generally studies tend to show that in-service courses do not have the impact which might be expected because for one reason or another teachers do not put what they have learned into action. This is partly a responsibility for in-service trainers and partly a responsibility for management within the school. Much work in courses needs to include a stage which looks at the implications for the classroom.

The experience of TRIST suggested that the most effectively delivered training has

1 involved teachers in pooling their expertise
2 offered a chance to approach common problems
3 offered tested strategies to tackle these problems
4 offered instances of existing good practice as exemplars
5 simulated real school scenarios under training conditions
6 employed a variety of delivery methods.

This adds up to a statement that work needs to start with where the teachers actually are and use their classroom experience as material to work on. A course on evaluation and record-keeping, for example, might start by listing all the kinds of records that the teachers present actually use and can think of. There might then be an opportunity to consider the purpose of records and to classify the records listed in a matrix according to the purposes of each. There might then be a place for a short talk on assessment and evaluation as a way into more detailed consideration of the particular records the school wishes to set out.

Activities which develop knowledge and skill

Knowledge and skill may be deliberately developed in a variety of ways and a school may use any of these as part of the in-service programme. The list which follows identifies activities which develop teachers but which are not part of a course.

Acting as a voluntary deputy

A number of schools make it possible for teachers to learn about more senior jobs by providing the opportunity to act as a voluntary deputy for a period. This is of value to the person doing the job as well as to the voluntary deputy. This kind of arrangement should be easier with local management of schools because it would be possible to pay someone for acting as a deputy for a period.

Action research

Action research starts with a teacher or teachers defining a particular problem and its dimensions in some detail, looking carefully at the relevant facts of the situation. This leads to the formation of an action plan to meet the situation which is then implemented. The outcomes of the implementation are then evaluated, leading to further planning and action.

John Elliot[22] stresses the way that the teacher involved in action research is concerned to question personal approaches in order to improve their quality and seeks to improve understanding of a particular problem rather than impose an instant solution upon it. He also stresses the need to take time for thought and reflection.

An action research group is best if it is representative of a wide range of people and it may be that a group could be created from more than one school and could include such people as advisers, educational psychologists, governors and parents, provided that these members come as working members and not as experts.

Coaching

It was noted earlier that this is known to be an effective method of helping *appraisal* people to learn, but is not much used. It could be used in the context of appraisal which involves observation of the teacher at work and therefore provides the opportunity for coaching. Similarly coaching could be used in helping teachers to acquire skill as discussion leaders or in making a presentation to a group.

Experimental work with children or young people

Any teacher can try out ideas with pupils and learn from the results. Work of this kind is more profitable when a pair or group of teachers work together to design and experiment and evaluate to results.

Giving a talk to a group

The preparation of a talk for a group of colleagues, parents or governors involves thinking out the ideas involved and this provides a development opportunity.

Job enrichment

There are a number of ways of making people's jobs more interesting. They can be given additional responsibilities for some interesting development; they can be asked to coach someone else in some aspect of their work; the jobs of a group of people can be re-planned so that they have the stimulus of something new to tackle. Another possibility is to make a careful study of a person's job, identify particular areas within it for development and provide for them.

Job exchange

There is a good deal of value in exchanging jobs with someone in another school. Working in a new environment with new colleagues and pupils is stimulating and suggests new ideas. This can be arranged between schools of the same kind or between a primary school and the secondary school it feeds. It enables a secondary teacher to get to know how the primary school works and possibly to meet children he or she will be teaching next year. The primary teacher discovers something about the way the secondary school works and can follow up children taught previously. Job exchange could be a matter of exchange for a week or so or for a term or a year depending on the particular things the teachers concerned offer to the school, their wishes and the views of the headteachers and governors concerned.

Job rotation

Where a group of people have jobs at the same level it becomes possible to plan for them to rotate from year to year so that they have experience of what is involved in all the jobs at that level. In a secondary school, this is something which can provide development for the senior staff of the school. In a primary school, the opportunity to teach new age groups provides development opportunities.

Keeping a diary

A diary of what is happening in the classroom noting specific things can provide opportunity for development.

Observation and discussion with other teachers

Teachers also learn from other teachers through staffroom discussion both formal and informal; observing pupils with other teachers; observing other teachers at work; talking with pupils and their parents; visiting other schools and being involved with other teachers in experiment and problem-solving activities.

Personal reading and study

A teacher may do a good deal of reading, selecting books which seem to offer something useful. This is given additional impetus if teachers are asked to report on their reading to groups of staff. All schools should try to provide a staff library which makes a wide variety of educational books available to teachers.

Preparing a report

The task of preparing a report, either from reading or from experience and investigation, has valuable development possibilities for the person undertaking it.

Receiving support and encouragement from senior colleagues

Although development is a personal matter depending on individual learning capacity, motivation and personality, the development of the teachers in any school is strongly affected by the headteacher and senior staff. Both the Bullock Report (*A Language for Life*)[23] and the Cockcroft Report (*Mathematics Counts*)[24] stress the importance of the head of department in the level of work achieved by the department; many other studies also make this point. One of the major reasons for giving the headteacher and senior staff a more limited teaching programme is to enable them to help and support other teachers.

Reflecting on one's own performance

Teachers may learn through their personal experience in the school and by studying their own work. This might include opportunities to talk over work with some experienced colleagues; provision of feedback on performance for a single lesson or work over a period of time; use of self-assessment techniques such as check-lists; using micro-teaching with a group of colleagues in which specific aspects of classroom technique are studied in detail and ideas tried out and evaluated; getting feedback from the pupils and so on. A good deal of this learning may be self-generated, but the school can do much to support and encourage it. Appraisal will make a contribution here.

Shadowing a pupil or becoming a pupil for a day

The opportunity to see what happens to a pupil in the course of a day is extremely valuable to teachers. There are two ways of doing this. A teacher can actually become a pupil for the day and take part in lessons with a particular group. This needs careful negotiation with the other teachers concerned, who may find it disturbing to have a colleague in the class. Alternatively a teacher can shadow a pupil for the day, following him or her to all the classes and noting what happens. These activities are valuable in giving the pupils' point of view. The opportunity to do this will also involve other teachers in making rearrangements to enable one teacher to be free for this exercise.

Shadowing a senior colleague

Teachers can learn about someone else's job by shadowing them for a period. This requires careful organization to free the teacher concerned, but the activity is very good preparation for promotion and if the school can organize to allow this to happen from time to time, it is useful. It is also useful for headteachers and deputies from different schools to spend time shadowing each other, and studying how someone else does the job.

Taking on responsibility and involvement in decision-making.

Involvement in management provides opportunities for acquiring management skills. These may include participation in decision-making activities; being given opportunity to exercise responsibility; being given opportunity to exercise interpersonal skills with adults; job sharing or job rotation; understudying a particular post for a period as part of deliberate staff development policy.

Taking part in group problem-solving activity

Every piece of work on problem-solving has some learning opportunity for some teachers. Any group formed to look at an aspect of the work of the school can involve some people who are there to learn as well as to solve the problem.

Teaching a variety of groups

The groups that a teacher has the opportunity to meet contribute to his or her development. A teacher who always has the brighter sets or the less able sets in a secondary school, or a particular age group in the primary school, is limited in development opportunities, and gradually becomes afraid of working outside his or her limited experience. Similarly teachers in single-sex schools need to consider the effect of this on their career prospects. It is part of the responsibility of the headteacher and the head of department to see that teachers are not caught up in this kind of limitation.

Triangulation

This involves observation of lessons from three aspects – that of the teacher concerned, that of an observer and that of the pupils. The idea is to discover how far what the teacher is intending to do actually comes over to those on the receiving end.

Visiting other schools

The opportunity to visit other schools provides teachers with a chance to see new ideas and consider their own ways of working in comparison with those of others. It is important to plan such visits carefully, so that the person visiting is very clear about the outcomes required. There should be opportunities to feedback after the visit. Although it is difficult to allow more than one person to visit at the same time, there are considerable benefits in doing so, since they have the opportunity to see more and compare notes about what they have seen.

Working with other teachers

Teachers learn from one another when they work together. Team teaching in particular provides a good learning situation for those taking part. A school may offer its less experienced members opportunities for working with other teachers to particular ends, seeking the solution to a problem or making plans for a piece of work. Colleagues may be observed at work and questioned. A teacher may listen to what others say, trying an idea here, a method or style there, gradually evolving a personal teaching style.

In all these learning situations, the teacher will be constantly taking in and sorting out new material and ideas, fitting them into an emerging frame of reference, digesting them and making them peculiarly his or her own.

3

The school and professional development

The school climate

Schools vary considerably in the extent to which they provide a climate in which the professional development of individuals can take place. This is related to various features of the school. In the first instance it depends upon whether the school is developing as an organization with a clear sense of overall direction. It is in this context that the development of individuals is most likely to take place.

McLaughlin[25] lists three important features of an 'ideal adaptive schools system':

1 Response to external pressures is proactive rather than reactive.
2 Internal demand for change is constantly stimulated and considered legitimate. Needs are assessed and problems identified on an ongoing basis.
3 The formulation of change proposals mobilizes political as well as organizational resources. Staff at all levels participate and develop a sense of ownership and commitment.

Bruce Joyce[13] suggests that

> where direct and clear training has been provided, where teachers have had the opportunity to generate their own ways of helping one another, the results have been consistently impressive, whether the focus has been feedback, skill and strategy training, curriculum implementation or staff reorganisation.

This emphasizes the need for teachers to be involved with the whole process of professional development. It is not something 'done to' teachers but a process of which they are a vital part at every stage. They need to be involved in the planning as well as the implementation of programmes of professional development.

Another area for consideration in looking at a school as a developing organization is the attitudes and values of the headteacher and staff. In a school which is developing there will be not only positive attitudes towards development but also positive and supportive attitudes towards individuals. Christopher Day, Patrick Whitaker and David Wren[26] suggest that there is a need for a school to consider the following questions in setting up professional development and appraisal:

1 How do values and attitudes affect relationships?
2 In what ways do the relationships express themselves?
3 How is power and authority managed in the school?
4 Which particular relationships affect the process of management?
5 What are the key features of the psychological climate of the school?
6 How do the fears and anxieties of individual teachers get expressed?
7 In what ways does conflict express itself and how does it get resolved?

They also note that

> successful management is very much a process of activating potential and providing space and conditions in which it can be creatively expressed.

A school which develops also tends to have a staff which shares a vision of what education is about, although there may be many aspects of the vision held by different people, particularly if the school is large. Nevertheless many values will be shared.

David Oldroyd and Valerie Hall[27] note that

> institutions with good staff development tend to have a collegial, participative style of leadership where heads and senior management
> - delegate significant responsibilities
> - encourage staff ownership of inset policies and programmes
> - invite open review of processes and activities
> - identify and use talented staff to lead inset activities
> - network good practice between groups in the institution
> - lead by example by themselves engaging in their own professional development

A headteacher coming to a new school needs to assess the view of education held by key members of the staff and look at how far there is any consensus as to what the school is about. In some cases, there may be a consensus which the headteacher finds unsatisfactory: he or she may need to work to change this, looking for ways in where there is some sharing of values on which development can be built.

The school development programme

Every school needs a development programme, arising out of school review
and evaluation activities in which everyone has been involved.

School policies

The development programme should be related to the policies which the
school has formulated about a number of the activities it undertakes. These
policies give a basis which the school has formulated about a number of the
activities it undertakes. They give a basis for making judgements about practice
and lead to aims and objectives which can be worked out in practice.

A policy is a statement of intent. In some schools there are policies set down
in the school handbook so that they are clear to everyone. In other schools
policies are not written down but are implicit in the activities which go on in
the school.

The creation of written policies has good opportunities for development in
the discussion which is involved in the formulation and later the reviewing of
the policies. A group of teachers coming together to try to formulate a policy
will gain a good deal and begin to acquire the commitment to the policy which
leads to school development.

School review

The school then needs a pattern of review which identifies areas for development. Figure 1 may help to identify these areas but it should be allied to careful
evaluation of each area under consideration. It is suggested that the importance
of each item is graded using the five columns given. This will help to identify
priorities in making a school development plan. It will also make a contribution to needs assessment for professional development.

The process of reviewing the school is important from many points of view.
People generally are increasingly aware of the need for schools to be accountable to parents and their community. It is therefore important to be aware of
the details of weaknesses and problem areas and to tackle them. Teacher
appraisal involves evaluating the work of teachers and this is more likely to be
acceptable to teachers if it is seen as part of the total process of reviewing the
school.

School review also has considerable opportunities for professional development and all teachers need to be involved in it in some way. In taking part
teachers become more analytic about problems and should become inventive
in thinking how to tackle problems. In surveying different aspects of the work
of the school they become aware of what is happening more widely. They also
learn about some of the tools of evaluation.

Figure 1 Identifying priority areas for a school development plan

Tick the column which most nearly indicates the state of this item in the school at the present time

TEACHING AND LEARNING	++	+	av	−	− −
Specific aspects of curriculum English Mathematics Science History Geography Languages Art Physical education Music Technology Religious education Other studies					
Teaching approaches Extent to which pupils are stimulated Variety of approach Match of work to pupils Provision for the full range of pupils Use of first-hand experience Class management					

Learning skills and behaviour
Pupils' ability to
  study independently
  make and check observations
  classify, order, sort out ideas and make
    generalizations
  ask questions
  find out from books
  reason
  generate ideas and carry them through
  make and test hypotheses
  solve problems
  evaluate					

Social learning
Pupils' ability to
  behave in ways which are socially acceptable
  work with others to an agreed end
Pupils' development of
  social competence
  moral behaviour
  ability to take responsibility
Pupils' involvement in running the school					

Preparation for adult life Sex education Education for parenthood Careers education and preparation for working life Education for citizenship					

ORGANIZATION	++	+	av	–	– –

Overall organization
Teacher deployment
Grouping for learning of
    pupils generally
    most able pupils
    least able pupils					

Arrangements for curriculum planning
Provision of appropriate documents
Curriculum planning arangments
Curriculum continuity
    pre-school to school
    year to year
    teacher to teacher
    primary to secondary school
    on from secondary school
Provision for exceptionally able pupils
Provision for pupils with special needs					

Grouping for learning Pupils generally Most able pupils Least able pupils					

Use of time
Timetable arrangments
Use of time by teachers
                    pupils
                    office staff
                    other staff
Time spent on different activities					

Use of material resources - books, equipment *materials, space*					

MANAGEMENT	++	+	av	−	− −
Arrangements for curriculum co-ordination and planning					

Staff performance and development
Performance of
    classroom teachers
    heads of year/pastoral posts
    heads of department/co-ordinators
Quality of staff development programme
Effectiveness of preparation for management
Effectiveness of induction arrangements
Effect on work of the school
Effect on individuals
Effectiveness of appraisal system					

Planning for change					
Decision-making Effectiveness Involvement of staff Involvement of pupils					
Use of money Division between different budget heads Cost per pupil Cost per teacher Method of making decisions about spending					
Administration Effectiveness of day-to-day running Routines, systems, returns, records correspondence					
Pastoral care Role of class/form teacher Effectiveness of class/form teachers Maintenance of pupil records Use of pupil records					
Environment Quality of environment State of environment Pupils' care of environment					

MANAGEMENT *(Continued)*	++	+	av	−	− −

Communication with
    teaching staff
    other staff
    pupils
    parents
    governors
    contributory schools
    continuation schools/colleges
    employers
    community
    LEA					

Relationships with
    parents
    governors
    LEA
    contributory schools
    continuation schools/colleges
    neighbourhood and community
    employers
Public image of school					

Assessment and evaluation
Arrangements for evaluating
    overall curriculum
    teaching approaches
    match of the curriculum to individuals
    individual progress
    record keeping
    internal tests, examinations
    external examination results
Arrangements for evaluating
    organization
    administration
    discipline
    planning
    communication
    staff selection
    staff development
    evaluation systems					

Sources: Adapted from lists in Joan Dean (1985) *Managing the Secondary School*[29] and (1987) *Managing the Primary School.*[28]

It is important in considering evaluation to have a programme for evaluating which ensures regular review of different aspects of the life of the school. This may be undertaken over a considerable period. The *Surrey School Review*,[30] for example, extends over four years with different aspects of the school reviewed each year. New developments also need evaluation built in so that time is allowed for this purpose.

Teacher involvement in the development plan

Finally in considering the development plan, a headteacher must ensure that teachers have been sufficiently involved in its evolution to feel a sense of ownership. It is also important that planning takes into account the workload which people already have and that plans include a realistic assessment of the time involved to put new ideas into practice.

The professional development policy and programme

The professional development policy

The headteacher and senior staff of a school are responsible for seeing that their colleagues have opportunity, support and encouragement to develop in their work. This involves the establishment and maintenance of a school policy for professional development.
    Such a policy might include statements of the following:

Overall philosophy and attitudes

A professional development policy might start by stating that it is the policy of the school to provide for the learning and development of all its staff in as many ways as possible.

The people whom the policy concerns

Professional development should generally concern everyone from clerical assistant to headteacher. This needs to be stated and accepted.

The possible professional development activities

There should be consideration of which activities need to be included in the policy statement, particularly any which are likely to give rise to concern, such as appraisal meetings or seeing teachers at work. The policy also needs to make clear that there are many developmental opportunities in the everyday life of the school.

Responsibility for professional development

The various responsibilities for the professional development programme need to be set out clearly so that everyone is aware of them. There is a clear overall responsibility for the headteacher and responsibility for teachers in management roles. There also needs to be someone with responsibility for co-ordinating and implementing the programme. In addition there needs to be opportunity for plans to be discussed by a group of staff as representatives and the organization for this needs to be part of the policy.

The way needs will be assessed

Every school should have a method for assessing professional development needs and this should be set out in the policy.

The part played by appraisal

The appraisal programme needs a policy statement in its own right, but its role as part of professional development needs stressing in the professional development policy. It is very much part of the process of needs assessment.

Provision for induction and probation

The policy needs to state the provision made for new members of staff whether they are new to the profession or simply new to the school.

Provision for management training

Every school needs to provide management training for its senior staff and for other staff in preparation for management roles. The policy needs to state this.

The way in which provision for individuals is built up

The programme for any individual teacher starts with his or her appointment. Once a teacher is in post there should be an interview to discuss developmental needs which should be reviewed during an appraisal interview each year. The policy should also state the school's provision for career interviews and counselling.

The way in which teacher's progress and development is recorded

A school needs to record the work of each teacher, perhaps by asking for a statement each year of groups taught and work covered and setting this alongside the appraisal record. Developmental activities ought also to be recorded.

Planning for succession

It is a common practice in industry to plan for the succession of people in senior posts, but very unusual in schools. This is partly that the methods of appointing people in schools do not give the freedom needed to train for succession, but there is no reason why a school should not train people with future posts in mind, provided that the people concerned recognize that they will have to compete for posts in the normal way and that there is absolutely no commitment to offer them any posts which may become vacant. It also helps if a number of people are clearly being trained, so that no one of them sees promotion as his or her right.

Shadowing

There are various ways of regarding this. One possibility is that of shadowing someone in a more senior post and taking over some of the responsibilities in the role of deputy on a temporary basis. Another is to provide opportunities for people to take on responsibilities of more senior posts for a period so that they get to know what is involved in the work.

The advantages of this kind of training to the school are considerable, because when vacancies arise there will be a number of people who have the necessary skills and abilities who know the situation in the school. This does not preclude the appointment of an outsider but improves the chances of an internal candidate getting the post. This is also an obvious advantage for the teachers concerned because they have a better chance of promotion both within the school and outside it.

The school programme

The overall picture of professional development is now one in which the school with its development programme is central, drawing on its own resources and on a range of activities from what is on offer round about to meet the identified needs of the school as a whole and its staff as individuals.

This is not quite as simple as it sounds, however, because initiatives for staff development at the present time do not come solely from the school, but are nationally and locally determined as well. The school must therefore build into its own programme the necessary training to provide for national and local developments. This may be provided by the LEA and may be part of a cascade system. One way of providing for this may be to determine only a section of the development programme, leaving other parts to be determined by others. Another possibility is to be sufficiently in touch with the national/local picture to be able to build in provision for these developments. Most schools will probably do a little of both.

4

The individual teacher and professional development

The need for professional development

The emphasis in teaching tends to be on caring for pupils rather than caring for the adults in the community yet it is essential that the adults develop in their work if the pupils are to achieve their potential.

We have already noted that we are in a period of unprecedented change and the process of staff development is part of the process of change. Most of the changes coming to schools from outside are requiring a change in teaching style, particularly where the secondary school is concerned. GCSE, TVEI are all demanding a different teaching style from that of former years. Although the National Curriculum is described in subjects at a time when there is a move to work across the curriculum, what is emerging from the working parties and the National Curriculum Council requires the same kinds of changes in teaching style as other developments. The changes involve more active learning on the part of the pupils and there is greater emphasis on the relationship between teacher input and pupil outcome.

In many respects teachers have moved a long way in a short time in accommodating themselves to the changes but there are nevertheless many constraints which affect their readiness and ability to change which must be taken into account in planning professional development within the school.

Teacher response to professional development

The SITE Project Evaluation Report (published in 1979)[31] found that only 6.2 per cent of teachers had attended a long course away from school; 26 per cent had been involved in other in-service courses away from school; 65 per cent said they would attend more in-service courses if they were focused on the particular requirements of their school; 70 per cent said that there were general problems for which whole-school INSET was appropriate; 73 per cent thought headteachers and deputies should use INSET for whole-school development; 82 per cent thought there should be a clear INSET policy, but only 13 per cent were in schools which had one.

The present situation is likely to be better than this, since many LEAs now require a staff development plan from schools, or expect staff development to be part of the overall school development plan. Nevertheless these figures suggest that teachers generally are in favour of school-focused in-service courses.

Christopher Day[32] notes three areas of constraint which affect the way teachers respond to professional development:

1 external factors affecting the climate in which professional development may flourish
2 social and psychological factors affecting response of teachers
3 the kinds of leadership roles and strategies used by the leader.

He notes some of the ways in which teachers avoid the challenge which change brings. They may

1 adopt the language of change but retain the old behaviour
2 become selectively inattentive to information that points to problems
3 change jobs or change roles within the same institution (this may offer professional development which is very effective or be a way of avoiding the challenge which a move to a different institution would bring)
4 make marginal changes to behaviour
5 use authority to elicit the desired behaviour from others, so that they conform to the desired change.

Day, Whitaker and Wren[26] point out that each teacher has

- *values* – specified and prized opinions
- *attitudes* – more or less settled modes of thinking
- *assumptions* – taken-for-granted ideas and opinions.

They also suggest that teachers share needs of

- *affiliation* – the sense of belonging (to a team)
- *achievement* – the need for a sense of 'getting somewhere' in what is done
- *influence* – the need for a sense of having some influence over what happens in the work setting
- *ownership* – the need for a sense of personal investment in the process of appraisal and its outcomes.

Any plan for professional development needs to take these points into account. Such plans also need to consider what is meant by professionalism and to use the teacher's desire to be professional as motivation. Eric Hoyle[33] defines a profession as having the following characteristics:

1 Practice is supported by theory.
2 There is a long period of training.
3 There is a code of ethics governing behaviour.
4 There is a high degree of autonomy.
5 There is responsibility for admission of members.

He also speaks of professionality as 'the attitude towards professional practice among members of an occupation and the degree of skill and knowledge they bring to it'.

All of this suggests that professional development is not a straightforward matter. Teachers have individual points of view stemming from their interests, values and assumptions and these affect their readiness to be involved in development whether this is for the school or for the individual. We have already considered the motivation involved in teacher learning in Chapter 2 and anyone in a leadership role in professional development must take this into account.

A. E. Wise et al.[34] suggest that

> to improve a teacher's performance, the school system must enlist the teacher's cooperation, motivate him and guide him through the steps needed for improvement to occur. For the individual, improvement relies on the development of two important conditions:
> ● the knowledge that a course of action is correct
> ● a sense of empowerment or efficacy, that is, a perception that pursuing a given course of action is both worthwhile and possible.

The teaching career

A study by Geoffrey Lyons[35] showed that fewer than half the teachers sampled had no clear perception of their career goal and method of attaining it. Over a quarter had a clear perception of the route they wished to follow from the point when they started teaching. Just under a quarter began teaching with no career map but developed one later. People who reached the top 'appeared to have strongly held career maps and a determination to acquire the experience necessary to progress through career compartments to an ultimate post'.

The process of professional development coupled with appraisal is likely to help many more teachers to develop a clear idea of where they want to go and it will be important in appraisal to help teachers to be realistic in their career goals. There will also be teachers who wish to stay in the classroom and continue to develop and improve their skills and these need supporting.

Professional development is a career-long activity. Initial training provides a starting-point but much has to be learned later. The early years in teaching involve learning about the teaching process; in the current climate of change, this learning is continuing for everyone because of the need to change teaching styles. Later years also bring for many the need to learn about management skills in relation to adults as distinct from classroom management skills and the programme should be such that teachers acquire such skills in advance of promotion. Experienced teachers may also need refreshment and encouragement to widen the range of successful teaching styles which they are currently using.

Staff selection

Professional development within the individual school might be said to start with staff selection in that what is needed by way of a development programme will depend on the skills and knowledge which teachers possess when they are appointed. Now that the process of selection is being handed over to governors entirely it will be the headteacher's responsibility to ensure that the selection process is thorough.

The Post Report (*The Selection of Secondary School Headteachers*)[36] notes that in selecting headteachers a great deal of emphasis tends to be placed on qualities of personality and too little thought is given to looking for evidence of the ability of the candidates to undertake the management tasks of headship. What is true of headship appointments is to some extent true of appointments at other levels in schools. Very few of those involved in interviewing will have been trained for this task; since the questioning for interviews is often given comparatively little preliminary thought, it may well be that the interviewing panel get only a limited view of what any particular candidate may have to offer.

The task of matching person to post involves collecting all the evidence available and offering the candidates evidence about the school so that they can make judgements about whether it is the place for them. The task of selection is then one of matching what each candidate offers against the requirements of the post.

It is important to have a job description and a person description for any post to be filled. The job description should contain the following:

1 title of post and salary
2 person to whom the post-holder will be responsible
3 responsibilities for
    teaching
    other activities
    pupils
    the work of other teachers
    ancillary staff
    resources – equipment, materials, etc.

The job description not only is valuable for the appointment of staff but also can become the basis of thinking about teacher appraisal.

A person description describes the kind of person who might be suitable to fill a particular vacancy. It should contain statements of what is required by way of

1 qualifications, knowledge, skills, abilities
2 experience
3 broad age group of potential candidates
4 special aptitudes
5 particular interests.

This is an internal statement useful in making the short list and in making the final decisions.

Thought is needed about the information sent to the candidates about the school. It should be as full as possible and should give some indication of the criteria for making the appointment as well as a description of the school and information about the post. The idea is to attract suitable candidates and put off unsuitable ones. It is also a good idea to ask for specific information in the letter of application.

The application should make it possible to make a preliminary match of candidates against post. The confidential report will add further to this and it is useful again to ask for specific information in requesting a report.

Finally at the interview itself, it is wise to plan the questioning carefully beforehand so that it elicits information about whether the person matches the job. If it is possible it makes sense to have more than one set of interviews so that more aspects of the work can be explored. A good deal of the time the candidates spend within the school should be devoted to getting information from them, rather than sitting waiting to be interviewed.

At the end of this process, when a candidate has been decided upon, it should be possible to identify areas in which the person chosen needs training and additional help and support. This should be one of the topics discussed at the first meeting with him or her after the appointment and a programme to match those needs should be built up. This may not be a formal programme, though it may have some formal elements. It is likely to contain elements of coaching and support from appropriate colleagues as the newcomer develops skill in the new post.

The skills and knowledge needed by teachers

Figure 2 gives in detail the skills and knowledge needed at all stages of teacher development. It could be used as a check-list for assessing individual needs (the right-hand columns are available for teachers to note their strength in the different items). This should identify which items they need to work at.

Figure 2   The skills and knowledge needed by teachers

GENERAL SKILLS	++	+	av	–	– –
Knows about 　　Salary and conditions of service 　　Person to whom responsible 　　Adults and children for whom responsible 　　Duties for which responsible					
Knows about 　　The school philosophies and policies 　　Patterns of responsibility and 　　　communication channels 　　Organization, discipline and pastoral care Routines and systems Patterns of assessment for pupils Patterns of overall school assessment Provision for the most and least able pupils					
Knows about The background of the pupils Information about individual pupils relevant for 　teaching and pastoral care Normal contact with parents Normal contact with other people, institutions 　and bodies					
Knows about Ways in which teachers' work may be assessed Staff development policy and programme LEA practice and available support for teachers					
Knows about Current developments in education					
Knows about The physical development of children and 　young people Their intellectual development Their emotional development Their social development					
Knows about Motivation for learning The need for learning to be active					

GENERAL SKILLS	++	+	av	−	− −
Knows about 　　The role of language in learning 　　The need for structure in learning					
Knows about 　　The effect of the group on behaviour					
Makes judgements about 　　Pupils' personality 　　Learning style in pupils 　　Pupils' experience and interests 　　Pupils' stage of development 　　Pupils' abilities					
Plans for class, group and individual learning *Creates a learning environment* *Creates learning situations* *Selects appropriate teaching methods* *Has good knowledge of teaching content* *Presents material to pupils competently*					
Uses questioning competently *Controls pupils competently* *Leads discussion in the classroom* *Communicates well with individuals* *Provides for the most and least able pupils* *Uses resources to advantage* *Identifies and solves problems* *Helps pupils to become independent*					
Makes long-term plans for classroom work					
Is able to use a range of assessment techniques *Assesses* 　　Progress of individuals and groups 　　Process as well as output 　　Own work *Maintains records*					
Is competent in administrative tasks of 　　Form tutor 　　Classroom teacher *Maintains a programme of tutorial work* *Knows well each member of the tutorial group* *or class* *Is skilled at counselling* *Conducts interviews with parents competently*					

MANAGEMENT SKILLS	++	+	av	–	– –
Makes and maintains good relationships with adults					
Evaluates what is happening					
Analyses problems and seeks solutions					
Is skilled at drawing ideas from others					
Is skilled at drawing together the ideas others offer					
Identifies and articulates aims and objectives					
Organizes to achieve overall aims and objectives					
Makes long-term plans for department or school development					
Cares for and supports junior colleagues					
Provides for development of junior colleagues					
Is skilled in					
Presentation					
Interviewing					
Leading discussion					
Negotiation					
Managing conflict					
Is involved in staff selection					
Is a competent administrator					

Needs at different career stages

It will be clear from Figure 2 that the needs of teachers are different at various stages of their careers.

Induction

There is first a period of induction which applies to anyone coming new to a school, whether a teacher new to the profession or an experienced teacher. In a secondary school there are usually several people who are new each year and it is possible to provide a programme specially for them. It is much more difficult in a primary school: although there is less to learn because the organization is less complex, there are rarely more than one or two people new at the same time. Yet the primary teacher has just as much need of the information contained in an induction programme and it should be the responsibility of someone on the staff to see that the appropriate ground is covered.

In both primary and secondary schools there needs to be a designated support teacher for the newly qualified whose task is to counsel. This role offers development possibilities for the person holding it and it does not necessarily have to be someone very senior in post. Someone with a few years' experience who will provide a good example, be sympathetic and skilled in the counselling role and also be capable of running meetings for probationers, may be more acceptable to a young teacher than someone older. The important thing is that it should be someone in whom the beginning teacher can have confidence and trust. Teachers will need training in this role. In the final national evaluation report of *The Teacher Induction Pilot Scheme*, Bolam, Baker and MacMahon[37] record that only 53 per cent of teachers in this role felt that they had had adequate training for it.

The support teacher for the school may share responsibility for the newly qualified teacher with a head of department in a secondary school and it is wise for the responsibilities of both posts to be spelled out so that all the necessary support is provided. It may be that the classroom support is mainly provided by the head of department with the support programme the responsibility of the person holding the post at school level.

Time will be needed to see the newly qualified teacher in the classroom and offer advice and to discuss the work observed. The support teacher ought also to arrange opportunities for the probationer to see skilled teachers at work; if there is more than one newly qualified teacher group meetings should be arranged in addition to a course, at which they can discuss the problems they are encountering. The newly qualified teacher will also need additional time for preparation – probably between 5 and 10 per cent of the normal workload. He or she is preparing work and materials for the first time and this is time-consuming. There is also a need for time to see more experienced teachers at work and to visit other schools. In an Australian study of newly qualified teachers,[38] 82 per cent rated this as important. This study also found that the greatest area of concern for new teachers was the class with a wide range of ability. The next was teaching the slow learner. It is likely that these findings would be replicated if a similar study were undertaken here.

In helping new teachers in their work it is important to realize that they are developing a model of what the teaching process is about and a personal teaching style. This will be formed from the experience they have had of seeing other teachers at work, whether as pupils or students themselves or as teachers, and it is important that they realize that there are a range of alternative ways of working effectively in the classroom and that different teachers have different styles. New teachers come fresh to the classroom in the teaching role and may have new ideas which with support can be successful.

New teachers, whether newly qualified or experienced, need an opportunity to get to know the school building at a very early stage – ideally before the new term starts. They also need an early programme which deals with the day-to-day aspects of school life. This programme might include sessions on the following topics:

1 school organization and discipline
2 pastoral care arrangements and what is expected of form tutors or class teachers

3 curriculum information
4 records required of teachers
5 routines and systems
6 pattern of meetings and decision-making processes
7 communication arrangements
8 arrangements for special needs
9 duties expected of teachers
10 extra-curricular activities.

In 1983 the DES published an administrative memorandum entitled *The Treatment and Assessment of Probationary Teachers*.[39] There seems to be a possibility that the probationary period will be phased out officially, but the advice given in this memorandum is still highly appropriate. It stresses that probationers should be placed in posts which make it possible for their work to be fairly assessed, where they are teaching the age groups and subjects they are trained to teach. It has a number of things to say which are relevant to professional development. For example it suggests that probationers should be able to observe teaching by experienced colleagues and visit other appropriate schools. The probationer's own teaching should be observed and assessed by colleagues and LEA advisers: this should result in advice and support. There should be opportunities for discussion with other probationers whether within the school or elsewhere. They should be made aware of the criteria by which they will be assessed which should include

class management, relevant subject expertise, appropriate teaching skills, adequacy of lesson preparation, use of resources, understanding of the needs of pupils and the ability to establish appropriate relationships with pupils and colleagues.

They should

have the opportunity to discuss their progress with those responsible for the assessment in time for them to heed advice before a final assessment is made.

In addition to the kind of support suggested above, the new teacher, whether new to the profession or to the school, needs a fuller programme, going into some of the topics more fully than was possible in the preliminary induction programme. It should be remembered that people coming new to a job can take in only a certain amount of information at one time. As they start to do the job they begin to see the need for certain learning and this is the best time to provide the opportunity for it.

The full induction programme might be expected to include the following items (cf. check-list given in Figure 2, pp. 41–3).

Salary and conditions of service

Teachers new to the profession need to know about the salary scale and what is expected from teachers on the main professional grade. They also need day-to-day information such as what to do if they are ill or late and the meetings they are expected to attend.

Responsibilities

These will be mostly set out in the job description, but someone, probably the head of department in a secondary school or the headteacher in a primary school, should go through the job description with the new teacher to ensure that what is in it is understood.

The school philosophies and policies

These may be set out in a staff handbook but they should be discussed. Where there are several new staff this may be a topic for a meeting with the headteacher.

Patterns of responsibility and communication channels

New teachers need to know who is responsible for the various management tasks in the school. In particular they need to know to whom they should go with particular kinds of problems.

Organization, discipline and pastoral care

Every new teacher needs information about the organization of the school and the discipline system. It is also important in a secondary school to know what is expected from form tutors by way of pastoral care. In a primary school less information is needed and discipline and pastoral care tend to be much more informal. Nevertheless the new teacher needs to know what is expected of the class teacher and what to do in a case of serious indiscipline.

Routines and systems

Every school has systems for dealing with matters like registers, lunch, sick children, new stationery, etc. New teachers need information about these systems.

Patterns of assessment for pupils

This will become increasingly important as the Education Reform Act 1988 comes into being and the testing pattern planned is fully implemented. Ideally a school should have a policy for assessment which sets down how the school is assessing pupils and what is expected from the teacher. This may be part of an induction programme in a secondary school with further discussion with the head of department. In a primary school it will be a matter for discussion with the headteacher.

Patterns of overall school assessment

A school should have some patterns of assessment overall looking more broadly at its life and work. Many programmes for self-assessment have been published by LEAs and a number of schools are using the *Guidelines for Review and Institutional Development (GRIDS)*.[40]

Provision for the most and least able pupils

A school needs to have a policy about the provision for the most and least able pupils; this needs to be made available to new teachers.

The background of the pupils

Information about the social background of the pupils is important information for the teacher, although it is important not to make assumptions about children's ability because of their background.

Information about individual pupils relevant for teaching and pastoral care

Teachers in any school need to have certain information about individual children for whom they have responsibility. Some information about these children needs to be given to new teachers and they then need to be kept up to date with any developments.

Normal contact with parents

New teachers need to know about the ways in which the school makes contact with parents and the extent to which they will be involved.

Normal contact with other people, institutions and bodies

Every school has contact with people in various specialist roles. These include the LEA advisory service, the education welfare officer, the educational psychologist, the school doctor and nurse, the speech therapist and others. There will also be contacts with colleges of education and with various institutions providing in-service training for teachers. New teachers need to know about all these and to know their likely contacts.

Ways in which teachers' work may be assessed

As appraisal becomes the norm it will be necessary to talk to new teachers about the school's appraisal programme and what it involves. In the case of teachers new to the profession, they need to complete a probationary period at present: what is involved should be explained together with information about the way in which their work will be observed.

Staff development policy and programme

New teachers need to know what is available by way of professional development and what support for their own learning they can expect.

LEA practice and available support for teachers

There will be information about every LEA which will be important to teachers, who need to know about the local advisory service and what it offers, teachers' centres, the library service, contacts with the local education office and appropriate people to ask for over different issues.

Main professional grade teachers

Certain skills and knowledge may be expected of teachers in the main professional grade. These may be present already or may need further development; many of the items listed in this section will also be relevant for teachers new to the profession. If the list given in Figure 2 is used as a self-assessment questionnaire it will be easy to see which items might be the subject of in-service work.

Knows about current developments in education

Developments are coming so thick and fast at the present moment that all teachers are likely to highlight this area as one where they need further training. Developments like GCSE, TVEI and the National Curriculum have been and will be given high priority for training by LEAs and the DES; this item will vary from year to year according to the developments that are current.

Knows about child development and can apply this knowledge in the classroom

Teachers new to teaching need to learn to apply what they have learned in college to the classroom. Knowledge of child development is usually seen as being more relevant at the primary than the secondary stage, but knowledge of intellectual development and the stage of thinking a child has reached is very important in teaching older pupils. Children in the secondary school may also be limited in their social and emotional development and may need help from teachers in these areas.

Knows about learning

Teachers new to the profession need to be able to apply their theoretical knowledge of learning and may need help with this. They may need the opportunity to discuss the way children learn with an experienced colleague. All teachers need to be aware of the role of language in learning and the need for learning to be an active process which has structure and what this actually means in the classroom.

Knows about the effect of the group on behaviour

Control of a class depends upon using the group to control the individual. New teachers have to learn to do this and it is helpful if they can observe experienced teachers at work and have the way in which the teacher is controlling the group pointed out.

Makes judgements about pupils

As teachers acquire experience in the teaching they become able to make judgements about pupils' abilities, performance, stage of development and so on and develop skill in assessing what is a reasonable expectation from pupils at different ages and stages. New teachers have to learn to make such judgements. This is probably best done by discussing pupils with an experienced teacher. This would seem to be a role for the head of department in the secondary school and possibly a head of year in a primary school.

Plans for class, group and individual learning

Different teachers set about the process of planning in different ways and there would be much to be said for exchanging views about the best way of planning. Secondary teachers tend to plan for a class, rather than groups and individuals, although this is changing, but many teachers welcome work on how to plan and organize for group work.

Creates a learning environment

This tends to be a phrase used in primary but not in secondary schools, although a number of secondary school teachers now create an environment in their rooms which encourages learning. There would be value at both primary and secondary stage in discussing what is meant by a learning environment and how you create it and use it.

Creates learning situations

In a similar way it would be worth discussing what is a learning situation and how you create it and use it.

Selects appropriate teaching methods

All teachers can benefit from discussion about teaching methods. Ideally a teacher selects from an armoury of methods those suited to the pupils, the material and the context. In practice most teachers use a fairly limited range of methods whatever the situation and can usually benefit from extending their range. Exchanges of information about possible ways of teaching a given lesson could be extremely valuable. It would be particularly useful to undertake such a discussion with teachers from a secondary school together with one of its contributory primary schools.

Has good knowledge of teaching content

Surveys of what teachers would like by way of in-service courses nearly always include a substantial request for work on content, particularly from secondary schools but also from primary schools. This may be difficult to provide in school for secondary teachers except where there is expertise within a department which can be shared or where the department is sufficiently large to warrant inviting an outside expert. The more likely method of meeting this need is for one person from a department to go to a course and come back and inform colleagues about its content.

At the primary stage everyone is teaching more or less the same subjects so it may be possible to use a colleague who is more expert, to invite an expert in or to send someone to a course and use this for everyone.

Presents material to pupils competently

Work on this might include classroom observation by pairs of teachers agreeing to look at each other's work or it may be part of the appraisal process in the school.

Uses questioning competently

This too might be part of classroom observation, but it might also be discussed by a group of teachers and different kinds of questions considered. In particular it is important to consider questions which make children think rather than simply recall.

Controls pupils competently

This is mainly a topic for newly qualified teachers although there are experienced teachers who have difficulty in controlling children. It could be a useful topic for discussion at a meeting of newly qualified teachers. It could also be a matter for discussion following classroom observation at any stage.

Leads discussion in the classroom

There is more skill in doing this well than is often appreciated. It requires not only getting children to discuss, but also summing up and drawing together what they say so that it results in learning. Much could be learned from discussion following classroom observation.

Communicates well with individuals

This is another point to be observed in the classroom. The good teacher normally has a balance in dealing with the class, groups and individuals. Some important learning often takes place as a result of individual conversation with the teacher.

Provides for the most and least able pupils

Every group of pupils includes a range of abilities. The skilled teacher makes provision for pupils at both extremes of the ability range. This would be a profitable topic for discussion and sharing of experiences. There could also be some sharing of materials developed for these pupils.

Uses resources to advantage

Teachers vary a great deal in the skill with which they use such resources as overhead projector, video recorder, computer etc. A course run by the teacher with responsibility for resources, suggesting the varied ways in which different resources can be used, may be valuable to many teachers.

Identifies and solves problems

Classroom teaching is a problem-solving activity. The basic problem is that of how to get pupils to learn but many individual pupils pose specific problems for the teacher. There are also problems in how best to organize for pupils' learning.

All of these problems benefit from discussion with other teachers or from mutual observation of lessons.

Helps pupils to become independent

All teachers should aim to make pupils independent learners, able to learn without help from the teacher. It is very easy for a teacher to make pupils dependent upon him or her; the teacher needs to give a lot of thought as to how they develop independence. Once again these skills benefit from discussion and from lesson observation.

Makes long-term plans for classroom work

It is easy to make teaching a day-to-day affair, although the National Curriculum is encouraging teachers to look ahead. It is important at every level to plan for the whole school year and to look at how these plans fit with the pupils' total experience within the school. This can be discussed by groups of teachers and long-term plans can be made by year groups in the primary school and departments in the secondary school.

Is able to use a range of assessment techniques

A teacher needs to be able to use different techniques of assessment, including observation, check-lists and testing of different kinds, both standardized tests and home-made tests. It is necessary to know a good deal about making observation reliable by undertaking it on more than one occasion and valid by careful selection of what is observed. Similarly a teacher needs knowledge of what tests actually tell one and how to interpret the results. This knowledge will be particularly important in relation to the national testing programme.

   Most schools will need a substantial programme of work on assessment for their teachers as national testing is implemented.

Assesses progress of individuals and groups

There has recently been a great deal of discussion about assessment, particularly in relation to the National Curriculum. Many secondary schools now feel that it is no longer adequate to allocate a general grade for work in a subject and much more thought is being given to the components which represent a pupil's progress. In the primary school it is now necessary to grade progress in a way which has not been necessary before, because of the grading system in the National Curriculum. At both levels a good deal of work is needed on how grading will be done.

Assesses process as well as output

The demands now being made for teacher assessment are concerned not only with what the child can do but also with what a child understands. This is much more difficult to assess. Teachers also need to assess the learning process going on in their classrooms as well as the output of the children.

This is a topic for teacher discussion, testing out of ideas and classroom observation.

Assesses own work

Every teacher assesses his or her own work to some extent. The difficult thing is to keep one's critical faculties sharp in relation to one's own work. This will be assisted by appraisal and by classroom observation.

Maintains records

Record-keeping has also changed a good deal in recent years. The work which has been done in secondary schools on records of achievement has given the teacher a different role in making judgements about aspects of a child's development and progress. This work is likely to affect record-keeping in the future. Teachers will also need to develop skill in discussing records with parents, particularly where a child is not making good progress.

Both primary and secondary schools need to consider the records they keep for different purposes and review them from time to time.

The pastoral role

Most teachers in a secondary school and almost all teachers in a primary school are responsible for a class of children. In the primary school the task of getting to know and support the pupils in the group is easier because the school is smaller and the teacher will teach the class group for most of the time. In the secondary school the form tutor must not only know and support the pupils in the tutor group but also undertake a number of administrative tasks which require a particular range of skills and knowledge.

Is competent in administrative tasks of form tutor or class teacher

This is mainly a set of skills and knowledge needed by teachers new to the school.

Maintains a programme of tutorial work

Most secondary schools now plan some tutorial time during which there is a programme of tutorial work. Leslie Button[41] suggests the following should be the basic concepts for the programme for the five years of secondary schooling:

1 the pupil's place in the school
2 the pastoral group as a small caring community
3 relationships, the self and social skills
4 communication skills
5 school work and study skills
6 academic guidance and careers education
7 health and hygiene
8 personal interests.

This requires a good programme of in-service education, especially where newly qualified teachers are concerned, since the pastoral care programme is something few teachers are trained for.

Knows well each member of the tutorial group or class

This is necessary knowledge for both primary and secondary teachers, although it is much easier for the primary teacher to know the class. It is helped if there is discussion of each pupil with a colleague. This helps the teacher to identify any pupils who should be better known.

Is skilled at counselling

Counselling is an essential part of the role of the form tutor. It is not a skill which comes automatically and teachers, because they are used to giving information, are inclined to tell children what to do instead of leading them to work out their own solutions. There is a case for training sessions with a skilled counsellor which include role-play.

Conducts interviews with parents competently

Interviewing parents is another skill for which teachers are not trained initially which is becoming increasingly important with the advent of national testing. It should be discussed by the whole staff and role-play exercises should be offered to give practice.

Management skills

Teachers also need management and leadership skills. Some of these are needed in the classroom, but many of them are needed in management roles within the school. Elizabeth Ballinger[42] suggests that needs arise for managers from the following:

1 The demands of the post the manager or leader currently holds, which will differ according to whether the post is middle or senior or top management.
2 The leader's perceptions of his or her own professional strengths and needs

(note the importance of appreciation of weakness, inexperience and failure as a component of personal development).

3 The leader's perception of the demands of the next post.

4 The changing needs of the school.

The check-list given in Figure 2 (p. 43) includes a list of management skills. Ideally teachers should acquire the appropriate management skills before they are promoted into management roles, so that they are prepared for what they are expected to do. These skills, basic to good management, are now discussed in more detail.

Makes and maintains good relationships with adults

It is essential for people in management roles to be able to get on with other adults. Skill in dealing with colleagues will affect the success with which any manager can work. This is not an easy skill to train and it is most likely to be trained through the appraisal process and by coaching, although there is much about relating to adults which can be learned generally.

Evaluates what is happening

A major task of anyone in a management role is to evaluate what is happening in the work for which he or she is responsible. Details of types of evaluation are given in Chapter 12.

Analyses problems and seeks solutions

Management involves problem-solving. There is a certain amount of straight-forward learning about problem-solving which can be offered. It involves a number of steps such as the following:

1 collect the facts

2 find out how people feel about the situation

3 identify the objectives

4 generate possible solutions

5 review the solutions and select the most promising

6 put it into action

7 evaluate the outcome.

Is skilled at drawing ideas from others

Good leaders do not attempt to produce all the ideas themselves, although this may be useful from time to time. The human brain is limited in the ideas it can have at any one time and a group of people can produce more and possibly better ideas than one individual. It is also generally acknowledged that people are most committed to ideas they have thought out for themselves, so skill in getting people to do this is needed.

This is partly a matter of a leader's skill in relating to people so that they feel comfortable with him or her. Leaders who find it very difficult to get people to produce ideas should look at how they receive ideas which others put forward. Good leaders make people feel that their ideas matter by the way they receive them. It could be helpful to get feedback and possibly coaching from a colleague following a session in which there has been an attempt to get ideas from others.

Is skilled at drawing together the ideas others offer

Once people have offered some ideas the leader needs to be skilled at weaving them together so that they can be used. This is part of the process of leading discussion and part of a more long-term process of using suggestions from other people.

Identifies and articulates aims and objectives

Leadership involves having a sense of direction. Part of the task of being a leader is to translate the ideas people offer into aims which provide direction. Aims then need to be turned into objectives, which are discrete tasks which can be seen to be achieved. A manager should to some extent do this by involving other people so that they feel they own the aims and objectives: leadership involves helping them to arrive at aims and objectives. The leader will probably need to be the person who actually puts the ideas into words however.

Organizes to achieve overall aims and objectives

It is a leader's task to make it possible for colleagues to achieve the aims and objectives which have been agreed. This involves satisfactory planning and organization of the work in hand and good management of the resources available. It also involves checking that people are actually achieving the objectives and moving towards the aims agreed. Some of this will be part of the appraisal process.

Makes long-term plans for department or school development

Good management involves long-term aims and planning over a period of two or three years so that a series of objectives are met. Pupils' education should have a coherent pattern over their years at school and teachers therefore need to see their work stretching over a substantial period. The development of teachers is also a long-term process in which a manager may need to organize so that each individual gains a variety of experience over time. The management of resources also needs to be long term so that collections of appropriate material are built up over a period.

Cares for and supports junior colleagues

Management involves responsibility for other people and this should be supportive. A teacher should feel able to turn to the person responsible for his or her work for help with problems and should feel that this person cares.

Provides for development of junior colleagues

Part of the caring process is development. Every manager is responsible for the development of the teachers for whom he or she is responsible. This means observing teaching and offering suggestions, talking over work and children, discussing possible in-service activities, ensuring that over a period the teacher in question has a variety of experience, is offered coaching where necessary and generally seeing that the teacher is increasing in skill. This is particularly necessary with inexperienced teachers but it is also necessary to find a way of helping experienced people to develop, perhaps by discussing work and children.

Is skilled in presentation

Every teacher should become skilled at presentation in the classroom. This does not necessarily mean becoming skilled at presentation to adults and a teacher in a management role may have to learn to do this. It is useful for a teacher attempting to develop presentation skills to ask a colleague to listen critically when he or she is making a presentation.

Is skilled in interviewing

Interviewing in the sense of having a conversation with a purpose is frequently necessary for a manager. A leader may have to spend time finding out what someone is doing, help him or her with a problem, deal with a discipline matter and much else and there is a good deal of skill involved in this process. Much that is said in Chapters 8 to 10 on appraisal applies here.

Is skilled in leading discussion

Leading discussion is a very positive activity where the leader can make a great deal of difference to the usefulness of the group. Advice about this is given in Chapter 5.

Is skilled in negotiation

Managing people means negotiating about many different things. Allocation of work and resources is often a matter for negotiation. The groups people teach may need to be negotiated. Various duties may need negotiation.

Negotiation is partly a matter of the way a leader asks people to do things. One manager will allocate activities with no disagreement because he or she has the art of asking persuasively. Another will find people arguing about almost everything because of the way the request has been made.

Negotiation is also sometimes a matter of getting two people with conflicting viewpoints to agree. It then becomes a task of finding common ground and seeking out how much each person concerned is prepared to give.

Is skilled in managing conflict

This is one aspect of negotiation. Conflict may be a matter of territory, whether physical or job territory. In this case it may be solved by trying to get agreement to boundaries. The conflict between jobs may be solved by sorting out job descriptions. Physical territory conflicts require rules for using the territory which are agreed by all parties.

It may also be a matter of philosophy where people have different views of what the educational process is about. This is much more difficult. Sometimes discussion will lead at least to some understanding of different views but sometimes it will lead to deadlock. It may then be a matter of finding a way of dividing work which allows for the differences in philosophy or of making a ruling about what is to happen – though this is the least satisfactory way of solving the problem.

Sometimes it is possible to allow people in conflict to pursue their views and to see what the outcomes may be.

Is involved in staff selection

Selection of staff involves one particular kind of interviewing but a good deal more besides. This is detailed on pp. 39–40.

Is a competent administrator

Any manager in school today needs to be competent in managing records, finance and general administration. It will also be necessary for headteachers and senior managers to know much more than they have done hitherto about personnel matters.

Teachers with breaks in service

One further group may be present on a school staff, usually as individuals or in very small numbers, and these are the teachers who have had a period out of teaching, usually to start a family. These teachers will find many changes in schools since they were last teaching and will need help and support in catching up with what has happened.

Some LEAs run specific courses for returners, but in most schools it will be a matter of individual coaching and counselling and using the opportunities which are available. The following will need to be covered:

1 the Education Reform Act 1988 and the National Curriculum and its implications for work in the classroom
2 information technology and its implications for the classroom
3 teacher appraisal and what is involved in it
4 the whole-school approach to special needs
5 language across the curriculum
6 the teaching of technology and science (primary)
7 GCSE and the changes in teaching methods which it requires (secondary)
8 TVEI and its implications for the classroom (secondary)
9 records of achievement and what is involved in producing them.

It will be helpful to teachers in this position if they can observe experienced teachers at work using some of the changed teaching methods. They will also need to do some appropriate reading and will require guidance as to what is needed.

5

The professional development programme

Organization

If a school is to provide for the development of all staff and also for the school as a whole, a complex plan and programme is needed, which demands very careful organization. We have already noted the importance of making everyone feel involved in the process of professional development and this means that there must be consultation at every stage.

It follows from this that the professional development programme is most likely to be successful in a school where there is an open style of management and trust between colleagues, where it is usual to ask questions and seek answers and where professional development is seen as normal practice which is built into the timetable and overall organization of the school.

If staff are to be involved in a large school, it will be necessary to form a professional development committee representing the staff which will act as a steering group for the programme. Such a committee should involve teachers at every level including those newly qualified. It may be formed by inviting particular teachers to take part, by election or by open invitation to anyone interested. In the latter two cases, it will be important to co-opt members if the committee is not fully representative of the staff. In a small secondary school and in most primary schools, the whole staff may be involved.

Schools will also need to decide what opportunities for professional development should be offered to non-teaching staff. In general little thought has been given to the needs of technicians, secretaries, caretakers, cleaners, dining-room and kitchen staff, although LEAs have often done a good deal about kitchen staff. If a school decides that there is a case for involving them in their own development it will be necessary to decide whether they should be represented on the committee. One of the problems about this is that their needs will be different from those of teachers and it may be time wasting for them to sit through discussions about teachers' needs. It may be better to have a separate group representing the non-teaching staff and create a different programme for them.

One county LEA, quoted by Oldroyd and Hall,[27] gives a useful list to its schools of some of the characteristics of successful INSET committees in secondary schools. They

1 are no larger than fifteen in number
2 represent a cross-section of age, seniority, gender and specialism
3 are chaired by the staff development co-ordinator
4 themselves undergo some form of induction to the skills involved
5 work actively to seek the views and opinions of those they represent
6 are conversant with the whole school curriculum and the school's development priorities
7 are fully briefed on externally provided INSET provision in the LEA
8 place individual staff development needs within the context of the school's development
9 recognize staff needs that do not fall within that context and seek ways of meeting them
10 plan annually within a three-year cycle
11 are fully conversant with budgetary limitations and INSET costings
12 are accountable through the headteacher and senior staff team to the staff as a whole
13 take an active part in leading staff development activities themselves
14 seek external advice and support
15 set goals clearly, consider flexible structures and monitor process and outcomes
16 operate a system of revolving membership to enable other staff to participate in turn
17 consult professional association representatives
18 take into account that a reasonable amount of the budget should be allocated to shared activities with primary schools and, where appropriate, co-operative projects with other secondary schools.

A great many of the items in this list also apply to primary schools, although in many cases the committee will be considerably smaller.

Professional development committee's brief

The professional development committee's brief may include some of the following items:

1 help to develop a climate in the school which is responsive to professional development activity

2 support the work of the professional development co-ordinator
3 help to identify the training needs of the school and the staff
4 make recommendations with regard to development policy
5 make recommendations with regard to the professional development programme
6 ensure that there is adequate communication about professional development to all members of the staff
7 arrange for the monitoring and evaluation of all professional development activity
8 have oversight of the professional development budget
9 monitor and make colleagues aware of professional development opportunities available outside the school.

Help to develop a climate in the school which is responsive to professional development activity

Committee members should help to develop the right climate for development in which there is a positive approach to development activity. This is most likely to happen if there is good communication. Committee members should have a clear responsibility for feeding back the deliberations of the committee to groups of colleagues and getting their view to put to the committee. This requires an organization which makes this possible.

Support the work of the professional development co-ordinator

Professional development activity, including the chairmanship of the committee, should be led by a senior member of staff acting as professional development co-ordinator, who has professional development as a major responsibility. As more of the money available can be used as the school wishes, this post will be increasingly important; it will be part of the work of the committee to support this teacher.

One of the difficulties for the holder of this post is that a good many of the opportunities for informal staff development, such as those described in Chapter 2, are in the hands of the headteacher and management of the school. The opportunity to offer people particular responsibilities or particular groups to teach cannot be undertaken by the professional development co-ordinator. It will therefore be very important that the person concerned also works closely with the headteacher and management in supporting and developing the work of individual teachers.

Help to identify the training needs of the school and the staff

This is dealt with in detail on pp. 66–9. It is a very important part of the work of the committee and the co-ordinator. A good starting-point may be to survey what is happening in the school at the present time. This will include all the activities undertaken by the school as a whole and by individuals within it including opportunities for professional development possibilities such as the opportunity to teach different groups each year or responsibilities which involve new learning. A number of these were outlined in Chapter 2. This will widen the concept of professional development and the possibilities available to staff.

Make recommendations with regard to development policy

The school will need to develop a policy for professional development and the professional development committee and co-ordinator should play an important part both in suggesting suitable content for policy itself and also for recommending the ways in which it is implemented. The development of a policy is dealt with in detail in Chapter 3.

Make recommendations with regard to the professional development programme

The professional development committee and the co-ordinator should be responsible for the professional development programme. It is tempting to think that a school programme can be designed and in place very quickly. The process of needs assessment and the overall planning of the programme take considerable time and while a programme of sorts dealing with immediate needs can be up and running while the assessment of needs is being considered, the kind of programme the school will need eventually will probably take about nine months to a year to develop, except in very small schools.

It is very important that early events are successful, since they will affect the attitude of the staff towards the whole process of staff development. It is also necessary to plan well ahead for events involving outside contributors, many of whom fill their diaries at least a year in advance. Financial planning will also need to be undertaken well ahead.

Ensure that there is adequate communication about professional development to all members of the staff

We have already noted that each member of the committee should be responsible for passing on information to a defined group of colleagues. Communication may also involve providing such things as a special slot in regular staff meetings for reporting back on plans, a notice board for professional development information, including the agendas and minutes of the committee meetings and a weekly, termly or annual bulletin giving information. Every opportunity should be taken to interest and inform the staff about development.

Arrange for the monitoring and evaluation of all professional development activity

Chapter 13 deals with evaluation in some detail. Here it may be said that the committee should have responsibility for monitoring and evaluating what is happening in professional development.

Have oversight of the professional development budget

The committee may also be given the responsibility of deciding how money available for professional development should be spent, including making decisions about teachers' attendance at external courses or it may be responsible simply for making recommendations.

Monitor and make colleagues aware of professional development opportunities available outside the school

It should be part of the committee's responsibility to keep track of what is happening by way of in-service education outside the school, particularly in the local environment. They are then in a position to suggest external courses to teachers which seem to match their needs.

Planning the programme

State aims

The aims of the professional development programme should bear some relationship to the overall aims of the school (see Figure 3). They will probably be a development of statements such as the following:

1 To provide an opportunity for all members of the staff to develop their work.
2 To provide for the overall development of the school

Oldroyd and Hall[27] suggest the following:

1 increase the staff's knowledge of, and participation in, the school community
2 enable co-operation with fellow professionals
3 assist staff to co-operate in the planning of the school's curriculum, both overt and 'hidden'
4 recognize and support good practice
5 initiate and extend training which helps all staff to cater for the needs of all pupils
6 provide a caring environment in which praise and encouragement flourish
7 specify and evaluate roles and responsibilities
8 assess and develop teaching and management skills

Figure 3   Professional development: planning the programme

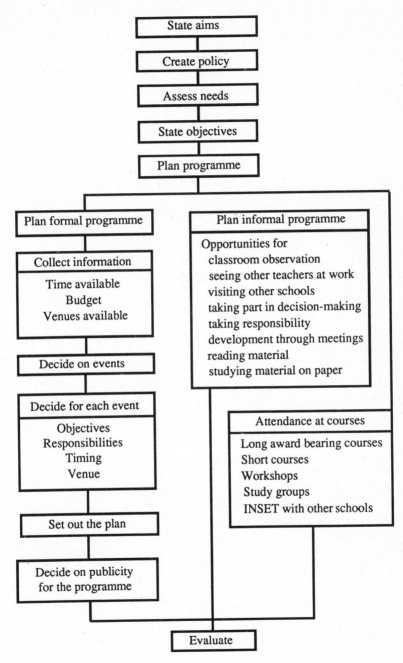

  9 help create job satisfaction and diversity of experience

 10 recognize and record the achievement and progress of all staff

 11 give each member of staff the right to an annual 'staff development discussion'

 12 facilitate staff's career development, both within and beyond the school

 13 keep staff up to date with educational developments

 14 encourage participation in external in-service training, and extend and amplify this in a school-based training programme.

Create policy

Suggestions about the formation of a professional development policy were given in Chapter 3. It was suggested above that a policy may well be something developed by the professional development committee for discussion by the headteacher and senior staff or by a wider staff group. Alternatively it may be devised by the headteacher and senior staff and discussed by the committee. The programme must then reflect the policy.

Assess needs

The next task for the committee is to assess needs, both for the school and for the individual teachers and other staff.

It is very important in assessing needs to make teachers feel that they are fully involved. Ben Kerwood and Simon Clements[43] suggest that

> The message teachers should receive is that it is their own perception of their needs which is the starting point; that they are being trusted to formulate their own problems; that they are being valued as the principal resource, that they are being given the power to manage their own learning and develop their own solutions. . . . The confidence that this realisation brings to the staff enables them to look for expert and theoretical help from outside when they need it and to be more open in the way they approach their work and their problems, evaluating, appraising and counselling one another and sharing ideas and successes.

The Manpower Services Commission *Summative Report on the TRIST Scheme*[44] concluded that

> A key factor in the success of needs identification exercises at school/ college level was the extent to which INSET was embedded within a clear curriculum framework; where staff had been involved in the formulation of curriculum policies they were more likely to see how their personal needs fitted into the overall pattern of development within their institution.

There are a number of questions to consider in planning needs assessment: the following may be helpful.

What information is needed to design an effective school development plan and programme?

If the programme is to be effective, this means it must enable teachers and others to do their work more effectively. It therefore follows that assessing needs involves identifying areas in which it is possible to improve performance. Individuals and groups can help to do this by saying what they feel are the areas in their work which need improvement, but these may not be the same as the areas that actually need improving. Some experienced teachers may find it difficult to accept the idea that any part of their work needs development, although the many changes at the present time may make the need for development easier to accept. It is part of the task of those undertaking the appraisal of colleagues to try to help them to identify areas of weakness of which they are not aware so that suitable opportunities can be sought for development.

What are the best sources of that information?

There are three possible sources of information: what people say they need, documentation which identifies needs, and observation of needs. All three should play a part in the needs assessment programme.

What are the best ways to obtain the information from these sources?

There are a number of ways in which information can be obtained:

1 Initial **discussions** with a teacher new to the staff. Once a teacher has joined the staff there should be some discussion with him or her to identify some specific areas in which the teacher wishes to learn.
2 Individual teachers can be **interviewed** to discuss their needs. This may follow completing a questionnaire or may be instead of a questionnaire.
3 Individual teachers may be **observed** to identify their needs. This might be part of the appraisal programme or, in a secondary school, a headteacher or deputy head might note that some heads of department needed work on inter-personal or other management skills.
4 A **questionnaire** can be circulated to staff to assess individual needs. The list of individual skills in Chapter 4 could be used for this purpose or a questionnaire could be compiled by the school. The best way to ensure returns from this is probably to distribute it at a full staff meeting and allow time during the meeting for it to be completed so that it can be collected. Alternatively it can be distributed for people to complete and return in their

own time. This may mean that some questionnaires are not returned. It may then be necessary for the teacher with responsibility for professional development to discuss needs with each teacher individually in the light of the findings of the questionnaire.

5 **Appraisal** should lead to an assessment of the needs of individuals. It will be necessary for the person appraising, with the permission of the teacher concerned, to pass on information to the professional development co-ordinator.

6 **Job descriptions** may give rise to INSET needs. This is linked to appraisal where job descriptions may be part of the discussion. Individual discussions with teachers may involve discussion of their job descriptions and any aspects of the tasks within them which require further training.

7 A **questionnaire** may also be used to assess school needs.

8 A **staff conference** can be devoted to assessing school needs.

A conference must be well structured if it is to be effective. The list of school needs in Chapter 2 could be used as a basis for assessing the areas in which staff feel the school could be improved. There is also some other useful material. The *DION Handbook*[45] is designed to help a staff identify development needs. *Sigma*[46] is another scheme for helping a school to assess needs. The use of a number of the school review documents published by LEAs should lead to assessments of areas where work needs to be done. The GRIDS material[40] leads a staff into thinking about needs for development. The LEA documents and the GRIDS material need longer than one conference, however.

A different way of doing this is to work in groups listing on large sheets of paper what people think are the main development needs of the school and then discuss these.

Another possibility is to take a series of questions:

1 What are our current strengths?
2 What are our current weaknesses?
3 What are the implications of these for professional development?
4 What priorities for INSET does this suggest?

What is the best way to analyse the information discovered as part of the needs analysis?

This needs to be considered before the information is gathered, so that problems are avoided. This is particularly important if a spreadsheet or database is to be used, but still important if information is to be compiled manually. It is extremely easy to obtain information in such varied forms that it is difficult to draw conclusions from it. It is also sensible when a questionnaire is to be used to try it out with a few people before using it generally. This provides a check on whether there are questions which can be misunderstood or misinterpreted. Even the most experienced compilers of questionnaires find that people misinterpret what seems to be clear. This also gives an opportunity to try out ways of analysing the information.

Whatever the method of identifying needs for the school, it is necessary to place them in priority order. If the ideas people have are written so that they can be displayed in a plenary session, everyone can list his or her first ten items from the lists and votes can be collected.

The individual priorities will then have to be reconciled with the school priorities. The first task is to look at what is common in the individual requests and to compare this with what has been identified at school level. A number of individual needs may be met in meeting school needs and it may also be possible to provide for groups of people needing much the same thing. Others may have to go outside the school for some of their requirements.

It is important that the needs identified both for the school and for individuals are kept in a form which can be referred to when necessary as the programme is built up.

State objectives

Once needs are known it becomes possible to identify objectives for the programme. If work has already been done on priorities by the whole staff group this makes the task of the committee and co-ordinator easy. If no work has been done on priorities then they must decide which items among those suggested should be tackled first.

Objectives are much more specific than aims but are related to the aims stated earlier. An objective should be stated in such a way that it is possible to demonstrate that it has been achieved. Examples of objectives might be as listed here:

1 to provide an induction programme for new teachers
2 to provide training in interpersonal skills as part of management training for senior staff
3 to introduce appraisal for some members of the staff.

Plan formal programme

Part of the planning for professional development will be a formal programme of in-service events. The committee will need to agree on the overall pattern of these events.

Time available for the programme

In order to plan the programme as a whole certain information needs to be collected. This includes the various amounts of time available for the formal programme.

The five professional development days

The provision of five days of closure for professional development is a big step forward in providing opportunities for teachers. It is possible that the LEA will wish to use some of these days, but the topics likely to be chosen are probably those which the school itself would need to choose since almost certainly the LEA will be concerned with seeing that schools are prepared for current developments. This is the one opportunity that schools have to involve everyone in development activity and it is therefore very important to use these days well. There is a need to create time for people to discuss fundamental ideas at length and the day closure is ideal for this. *Planning professional training days* by Bob Gough and Dave James offers useful suggestions here.

In planning day closures or any major piece of professional development, it is important to involve teachers in their own learning. Paul Bamber and John Nash[47] have written of the problems created when schools close for a day to learn about topics in which the teachers had no say. Trainers called in to help with such a programme believe that

> it will be participatory and aim to call on the skills and expertise extant in the school to enable the management of change.

The teachers, for their part,

> may believe that the visitor is an expert who will tell them all that they need to know about a given subject in a day. Their expectation is that they will be spoonfed information, the main purpose of which is intellectual stimulation, not change in the classroom.

It is clearly important to avoid this kind of situation and ensure that the activities planned involve teachers in developing their work with children. It is worth noting that there is often as much development opportunity in sitting down with colleagues to work out a record-keeping system as there is in listening to someone talk about record-keeping.

Any time which can be timetabled for staff development

Secondary schools need to give thought to ways of timetabling which release groups of teachers for developmental activity, particularly related to school and departmental needs. This may be release to attend a course outside the school or release of a group of teachers to work at particular development. The period after examinations can be particularly useful for this purpose. The following possibilities might be considered:

1 Are there situations in which slightly larger groups would enable a teacher to be released for developmental work?
2 Would a modular programme for some work enable a teacher to be released for one of the modules?

3 Could any of the time being spent in changing lessons be avoided, making it possible to release staff for other purposes?
4 Could any of the work where there are parallel groups be undertaken by one teacher with two groups, releasing the other teacher?
5 Could teachers be freed for development work while one year group is on work experience?
6 Is the examination period and the time following it being sufficiently well used?

Primary schools have more difficulty in making such arrangements because there is very little flexibility, but sometimes part-time staff and the headteacher can provide opportunities for staff to work together or perhaps one teacher can work with a larger than usual class to release other teachers. It is also possible to organize the school in rather larger groups, thus freeing time for some staff to do developmental work.

An after-school programme for interested groups

Many teachers are prepared to give time to their own development and to attend seminars or discussions on a regular basis with a programme planned in advance and well prepared by those running it. These may involve lectures or workshops run by staff members or visiting speakers; use of prepared materials with a staff group, e.g. tapes, slides, videos, prepared-in-service packages, etc.; viewing television or listening to radio programmes made for discussion by teachers, and many other activities. Some schools have found it valuable to arrange evening meetings which include a meal (usually put together by each teacher bringing a contribution). The teachers involved in this note that the social element in the evening brings them together as a group and helps their working together. They relax over a meal and a feeling of being part of a team is often generated, particularly in a small school.

Jean Rudduck[48] notes that the advantages of the after-school course are that people have time to reflect and try out ideas between the sessions and the course leader has time to modify the programme to match the group. The disadvantages are that teachers are tired after a day's work, they are not always free to come to every session and they have a tendency to lose the thread between meetings. In practice the programme has to be planned with these disadvantages in mind.

Rudduck found that such courses were particularly useful for disseminating information, as an arena for small-scale experiment with teachers trying things out between sessions, as a production workshop with teachers making materials for their work, as a clinic looking at problems brought in by course members and as a seminar for discussion of issues.

A residential course during a holiday or weekend

One of the best possible situations for development and fundamental discussion is a weekend away in a hotel where a pleasant venue contributes to the feel of the work. A weekend or part weekend at a course centre is also profitable if the conditions are good. Teachers tend to feel that if they are giving up their weekend, the course should be somewhere pleasant. Courses during holiday periods may pose fewer problems, but need booking a long time in advance if possible course members are to keep the period of the course free.

Such courses are expensive, but when set against the cost of supply cover seem less so. A course in a hotel needs rather different preparation from a course in a centre. A hotel that is used to providing for courses will set up the room, provide equipment as required and generally look after their guests. They will probably charge for the use of the room and possibly for the use of equipment, however, so it is important to clear with them exactly what is covered. In most course centres the course organizer will need to make rather more of the arrangements, but they will probably cost less.

Residential courses can make more impression on those attending them by virtue of the intensity of the experience. More can be fitted in because the evenings can be used as well as the day. They are particularly valuable for long-term planning activities because people can concentrate fully on what is required.

Budget available for the programme

In planning the programme it will be necessary to know what resources are available. These will then have to be allocated to different items. The committee needs to know the overall sum available to it and any constraints on its spending. It also needs to know what supply cover will be available. This is usually the most expensive item in the budget and it makes sense to plan to use supply cover as carefully as possible.

The budget will also dictate whether it will be possible to undertake any meetings at a venue other than the school, since this will involve paying travel expenses. The budget must also include an element for teachers attending courses or making visits.

Venues available for the programme

School premises are not always available for the use of the staff and it will be necessary to find out the extent to which others use the school and when it is available. As we have seen there are advantages in using a different venue from time to time and it may be valuable to find out what other premises are available.

Decide on events

Once the plan has been considered in broad terms it can be turned into the formal programme of events. This involves careful thought about priorities, both for individuals and for the school as a whole. It is very important that the headteacher and senior management of the school have a chance to comment on their own priorities before the programme is too far advanced so that everyone is going in the same direction. What is included will depend on what has been discovered as a result of the needs assessment process, but there are some areas of work which should be considered for inclusion.

The need for teachers to develop in their present role

Job satisfaction comes from developing the job one does. Many teachers will spend their careers in the classroom and need to stay enthusiastic and thoughtful about their work. A good deal of the programme should be designed for this purpose. Appraisal will also help this as will the classroom observation which should be part of the appraisal process.

Other teachers in management roles need the chance to develop their work in leading adults and this too should be reflected in the programme.

Future needs arising from school, local and national developments

At the present time there are major developments taking place nationally and these must play a large part in the school programme. These developments will gradually become absorbed, however, and there will be other demands from outside the school.

One of the problems about the demands from outside the school is that they often occur at very short notice and schools are expected to make a place in their planning for something which is unexpected. This can be upsetting. Schools need to leave space in their plans for the unexpected, not only from outside but also from inside. There should be some time allowed for development which is not tied to a particular topic until near the date, as well as a programme which is planned a long way ahead.

Not all the school's future needs are of this nature. It is possible to see changes in roll, for example, or reorganization or to plan to change the curriculum or the pastoral care programme in some way. These changes can be planned for and should be part of the programme every year.

Future needs arising from staff changes

While it is not customary in schools to plan for succession in the deliberate way which is used in some industrial settings, it is nevertheless a good idea to see that enough people are acquiring the managerial skills needed to succeed the heads of year or department, the curriculum co-ordinators or the deputy heads, so that when someone leaves there is a choice of well-trained people from within. Planning in this area should help to meet the needs of individuals to plan for their future careers.

The emphasis in staff development will vary according to the particular needs of the school at any given time and the particular group of staff in office. There are, nevertheless, some staff development activities which should be a permanent part of the programme, although the way they are conducted may change.

The first of these is induction. We noted in Chapter 4 that new staff, however experienced in the work, need induction into the particular school organization and systems. Some of this can be done by providing a programme on paper, but there is also a need for more formal provision covering the ground suggested in Chapter 4.

Chapter 4 also stressed the importance of provision for probationers. Probationer teachers do not complete training knowing all they need for their career and DES Circular 1/83,[49] which lays down a number of guidelines both for LEAs and schools, suggests that before taking up an appointment the probationer should have much of the information suggested in Chapter 4, such as useful facts about organization, staff, etc; notice of the timetable to be taught; copies of all syllabuses or schemes of work within which the probationer will be operating; information about equipment and other resources available for use; information about support and supervision provided by the LEA and the opportunity to visit the school to meet the headteacher, the head of department and fellow members of staff.

The Circular goes on to suggest that after taking up the appointment the probationer should be able to seek guidance from a nominated member of staff and the head of department, as appropriate (this too was discussed in Chapter 4). The person concerned will need training for this role. This may be provided by the LEA but may need to be the responsibility of the school. The Circular concludes by reminding everyone concerned with probation that

> In considering any appeal against dismissal by a failed probationer, industrial tribunals have no power to question the professional judgment of a probationer's competence, properly and reasonably exercised, but they do take great pains to discover whether a probationary teacher has been fairly treated during probation, particularly with regard to the support given, the conditions in which the probation has been served, e.g. the suitability of the post(s) occupied and whether the probationer has had adequate advice and warning on performance.

It is therefore very important that the management of a school ensures that probationers have the best possible start to their teaching careers.

All that has been said about new teachers and probationers will have even greater application if a school has on its staff licensed teachers or articled teachers. It is likely that special arrangements will be needed for training teachers coming into the profession by this route, but they will make considerable demands on existing staff.

Opportunities to reflect on performance and evaluation

All teachers need opportunities for reflection on performance and evaluation, work on classroom skills and management development. The trouble is that schools are such busy places that time for evaluation and reflection seems hard to find. The senior management of the school not only need to see that the organization is such that they themselves have time to evaluate and reflect but also must create time, opportunities and encouragement for others to evaluate. Evaluation must also be built into a large number of the activities of the school, particularly when anything new is being tried.

There is a sense in which we create reflection opportunities by giving people more rather than less to do. The department asked to make a statement justifying the inclusion of its specialism in the curriculum, or the primary school year group asked to state its aims and objectives and explain how they fit into the school aims or to undertake some similar activity with a deadline date, will somehow find time to do this if it appears to matter. In the process they will do some fundamental thinking about their work which they might not have done even if they were given a great deal of free time to do it. Similarly evaluation can be treated as essential at certain times of the year, perhaps linked to appraisal. The first task of management therefore is to stimulate and structure thinking by the questions asked and the demands made.

Reflection on performance and evaluation are further developed by teachers seeing each other at work and offering comment. The headteacher and senior staff have a role in doing this, but there is also value in peer group evaluation; if two or more teachers can come together and organize themselves so that they see something of each other's attempts to achieve particular things in the classroom, this too is valuable.

Training in management skills

Another permanent element in the programme should be management. It is unlikely that a school ever achieves the situation when everyone in a management role is fully trained in all the skills of management and in any case there will always be those aspiring to management roles who need training. There should therefore be opportunities in the course of each year for those in management roles and those aspiring to them to receive training. Some of these opportunities may be provided outside the school and it may then be a matter of directing different teachers to the opportunities available. There is also a case for in-house work, however.

Decide for each event

Objectives

Once events have been decided upon there is work to be done on each before it can be handed over to a subcommittee to put into action. The first task is to decide on objectives. These should be a clear statement of what each event is about, for example

At the end of this course, teachers will be able to set up and use a computer database.

Responsibilities

Each event should be the responsibility of one or more people and it should be clear what the responsibility involves. It should probably involve arranging the venue, including the provision of any equipment or materials needed, providing any speakers or group leaders, organizing any supply cover, organizing refreshments, seeing that the course is properly advertised to the right people and liaising with the headteacher and caretaker.

Timing

The committee will need to agree the timing of all the events in the formal programme, taking into account other events in the school year and the availability of premises.

Venue

The committee will also need to decide on the venue for each event.

Probable membership

Different courses will attract different groups of teachers: decisions will have to be made about which courses are to be available to everyone and which are for a particular group.

Budget

The committee must decide on a budget for each course which takes into account any costs for the venue and resources, speakers, travel, refreshments and supply cover. Those planning each event should have a clear idea of what they have to spend.

Figure 4 Network analysis for the professional development programme

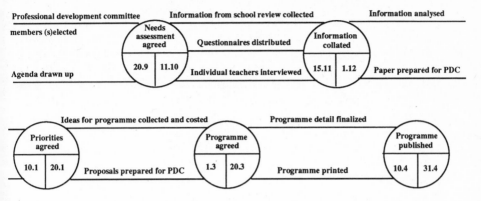

Set out the plan

Once the plan has been decided upon, it is important to set it out so that the relationships of different elements in it can be seen. It can be helpful to set it out on a year planning sheet so that the timing of each event is evident. It is also possible to put on such a sheet other major events in the school calendar. This will help to avoid unfortunate clashes of events and overloading of teachers.

Another helpful way of setting out plans is a network analysis (see the example in Figure 4). This is started by listing 'events', that is activities which take place at a single point in time, such as the course or conference itself or planning meetings for it. The circles in the network represent the points in time and the dates given in the lower half of each circle represent the earliest and latest date by which the event must take place. 'Activities' between the events are then put in and this provides a check-list of what is to be done for each event.

Decide on publicity for the programme

Once the programme has been designed, it is important that it is widely publicized. If possible every teacher should be given information about it. The professional development notice board should advertise in-service events and there might be a weekly or termly bulletin about the latest plans.

Plan the informal programme

While the formal programme is taking place there should be alongside it an informal programme for individuals involving activities such as those described in Chapter 2 using the day-to-day work of the school. All the normal work of the school has staff development possibilities, particularly that which involves decision-making. The distribution of the money available under local management of schools (LMS) requires careful thinking about what needs to be developed within the curriculum. Open days and parents' evenings can give rise to discussion about what it is important to demonstrate to parents about the school and the skills involved and knowledge required in talking with parents about their children. All special activities can offer someone a chance to develop skill in organizing. Experienced teachers may be used to support the less experienced in various ways and gain themselves as a result. Membership of working parties inside or outside the school provides development opportunities and this should be taken into account when forming such groups. The opportunity to teach different groups and to take part in cross-curricular activity is valuable. Shadowing or acting as deputy to a more senior member of staff as a development opportunity has much to commend it. Jobs can be rotated or exchanged. Extra-curricular activities offer opportunities for some teachers to demonstrate their abilities.

A great deal can be learned by visiting another school, particularly if the visit has a clear brief. This can be a useful part of any development within the school and teachers can be selected to visit different schools and report back. There are also a number of centres which specialize in different activities where teachers can go to see materials in a particular area of curriculum.

Both school and centre visits benefit if more than one person can go, though this may pose a problem for the school. It is helpful to be able to discuss with someone during a visit and in reporting back. Where teachers are visiting in order to implement something in the school themselves it is helpful to have someone to share discussion about the possibilities who has seen work in action elsewhere.

Most meetings can offer something by way of professional development if the agenda is not confined to day-to-day business but also includes discussion of more fundamental issues. Almost any topic can be slanted to provide such an opportunity. For example, discussion about an open day might include discussion about relationships with parents. Discussion about the Christmas play might include discussion about what teachers felt the children might get from it. Consideration of books to be bought could lead to discussion about the criteria for selecting books for the school or department and so on.

The major problem about using meetings for such topics is that of time, where decisions may be needed fairly quickly. However, with good planning it is possible to use the decision-making process to stimulate thinking.

Provision for teachers to develop might include the provision of specific written material and discussion. The staff handbook, policy statements, schemes of work, etc., provide information which all teachers need. There will also be papers prepared for conferences and meetings and papers produced as a result of professional development activities which will be valuable to individual teachers.

Every school needs a staff library and specific encouragement to teachers to undertake relevant professional reading. The pressure on everyone in education at the present time makes reading difficult to fit in and the school needs to encourage teachers to undertake it – perhaps by making a request to particular teachers to read a given book and report on it to colleagues. The staff library needs the same sort of selling to teachers as the school library needs for pupils. Books need displaying and talking about.

Attendance at courses

Part of the overall pattern of in-service education is the opportunity to attend courses locally or nationally. The co-ordinator of professional development should make a point of seeing that the school receives all the information possible about courses available and that this is made available to teachers. It may also be a good idea to try to link the list of courses with the needs individual teachers have expressed and to draw attention particularly to courses which appear to meet a given need.

There will also be situations where the school wishes a teacher to attend a particular course because the school needs the skills and knowledge which the course offers. Course lists should be scrutinized for courses which meet individual and school needs.

Part of the work of the professional development committee may be to decide how much of the budget can be used for individual course attendance as compared with in-school courses available to everyone. In particular it may be necessary to decide whether the school can afford to send a teacher on a long course, which will mean absence from the classroom for a period. Money also needs to be set aside for attendance at short courses.

It is not easy to reach a suitable compromise and it must be remembered that the cost of attending a course includes not only the course fees and perhaps residence.but also travel, which can be very expensive if the course is a long way away. Decisions about individual applications will then have to be reached in the light of the overall money allowed for this part of the programme in consultation with the headteacher and governors. Some of these decisions will not be popular. Decisions about the amount of the budget reserved for individual course attendance should be made widely known so that everyone is aware of what is possible.

Long award-bearing courses

The teaching profession has gradually become an all-graduate profession and there are now very few non-graduates. Many teachers gain, not only in the learning they achieve but also in their promotion prospects, by undertaking a higher degree or advanced diploma. Many higher degree and diploma courses are now closely related to the work of schools and the school from which a teacher comes should gain from his or her study. Such a course may require the teacher to be seconded full time or to spend some time each week at the course and further time working at home.

In discussing whether to second a teacher for such a course the headteacher and governors will need to bear in mind what it is likely to offer the school both as part of the course and what it offers the school long term, as well as what it offers the teacher.

Short courses

There will be teachers who want to attend courses for their own benefit and teachers whom the school wishes to ask to attend a course for the school's benefit.

Attendance in either situation should carry with it an obligation to give a feedback report to at least a group of staff and to do some work in the area under consideration.

Workshops and study groups

Teachers may also be involved with local workshops and study groups, possibly run by the advisory service or a teachers' centre and concerned with curriculum development or development of some aspect of the work of the school. These are often very valuable to those taking part and may include senior members of staff who feel that many ordinary in-service activities are for the less experienced. Usually the cost is little more than travel.

INSET provision with other schools

Shared work with another school provides new views and gives teachers the opportunity to hear how others work. It is particularly valuable to have some shared activity with contributory and transfer schools; in the case of a school which is part of a sixth form or tertiary college organization shared in-service activity with the staff there is valuable. There should be a good deal of joint planning of curriculum between schools which teach the same children at different stages and a joint programme provides opportunity for this. It also provides the opportunity to dispel some of the myths which one stage of education has about other stages.

6

Professional development activities

Planning a training event

The professional development programme is likely to be partly made up of a series of training events, which themselves include a number of different activities. This chapter is concerned with the planning of training events and the activities from which they are built up.

Training events require very careful preparation using the sort of pattern shown in Figure 5. (The material which follows is adapted from my book *Teachers Learning*.)[50]

State aims

The first question to consider when planning learning for other people, whether teachers or children, is 'What kind of outcome is required?' If the planning cycle described in Chapter 5 is followed those planning a particular activity are likely to be given the aims of the activity although they may wish to expand the statement given them.

Collect information

In planning a course a certain amount of information must be collected. Some of this is already decided, for example the date in planning for a day's closure; other pieces of information may come from negotiation by those planning the overall professional development programme, for example the money available. There will then be large areas in which those responsible for the course are free to plan as they wish. The list which follows can serve as a check-list of information required.

Figure 5   Professional development: planning a training event

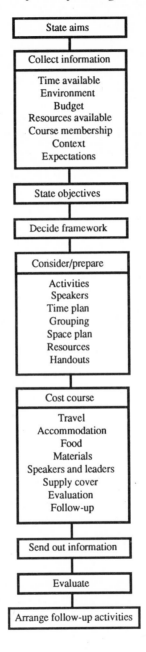

Time available

The time available makes some approaches more possible than others. For example a full day's course makes practical activities easy to arrange, but this is more difficult to arrange in an evening session when there is less time. In planning time it is also important to allow time for setting up whatever may be needed and for clearing up afterwards.

Environment

Much school-focused in-service work is school based and this can be an advantage. Nevertheless it is wise to check on the following items.

1 The number of people the rooms available can take comfortably.
2 The chairs and tables needed.
3 Power points, plugs, etc. in relation to the equipment likely to be used.
4 Sight lines and acoustics in relation to the kind of activity planned.
5 Any display facilities needed.
6 Arrangements for tea, coffee, meals, etc., their timing and their cost.

If the course is to be elsewhere and particularly if it is to be residential, the following additional items need to be checked.

1 Arrangements for parking.
2 Is the accommodation in single rooms?
3 Are soap and towels provided?
4 What times are meals?
5 Are there facilities for making early morning and late night drinks?
6 Can newspapers be purchased?
7 What are the costs, including any costs of seminar rooms and hire of equipment?

Budget

It is essential to know at the outset of planning how much money is available and what it must cover. In particular it is necessary to know whether it is to cover the cost of meals, travel if there is any, and supply cover, as well as the cost of any speakers and materials. Supply cover, in particular, is very expensive and its use requires a good deal of careful thought.

Budgeting for a single course needs to be seen in the context of the whole professional development programme which should be budgeted as a whole, allocating money to particular parts of the programme.

Resources available

The resources, materials and equipment needed for a given course should be carefully itemized in advance and checked over to see that they are in working order. Visiting speakers should be asked in the correspondence what they will need. Films and videos should be ordered.

Course membership

Most of the courses a school runs for itself will be open to the staff as a whole and planning must take place with this in mind. There will be some courses for particular groups, however. For example there may be an induction course for new members of the staff or a management course for heads of department. Decisions about course membership need to be taken at an early stage so that planning can be directed to the group involved and the appropriate numbers can be taken into account.

In a large school it is sometimes a good idea to have a series of invitation courses which make it possible to create groups which are likely to be cohesive. This needs careful explanation to colleagues with a promise that everyone who wishes will eventually be invited. When selecting groups in this way it becomes possible to mix people who are lively and forward-looking with others who are less so: this can mean that those who are less ready for change are influenced by their colleagues.

A further development of this is to join with another school. This makes it possible for a wider variety of views to become evident.

Context

Any course which is part of the school programme should be seen in the context of the whole programme. No course stands alone but is part of a plan to develop the school and individuals in certain directions. It is helpful to be able to demonstrate links between any particular piece of in-service work and the rest of the programme.

Expectations

It is useful to know what people coming to a given course are expecting to get from it. Those planning the course may have particular ideas, but unless the course satisfies its members' expectations to some extent it will not be successful. It is therefore very important to state clearly what the course is about. The information given in advance should attract only those people for whom it is intended. It can be useful to ask course applicants what they are hoping to get from the course, so that those running it are aware of the expectations of participants. People normally come to courses for some of the following reasons:

1 to learn something afresh or update knowledge
2 to get fresh ideas, improve practice, undertake new responsibilities

3 to compare their own practice with that of others in order to confirm, consolidate or improve
4 to seek for help in developing particular work.

State objectives

A short course, like a series of lessons, involves deciding on objectives which will help to meet overall aims. Aims are broad statements of intent. Objectives need to be stated so that they can be seen to be achieved, perhaps in the form of what people will be able to do after the course. For example:

> At the end of this course each member will have devised a number of ways of teaching towards the attainment targets at level x in the national science curriculum.

Not everything which people might learn can be set down in this way, but it is helpful in planning to try to set down as much as possible in this form. It makes the planning of activities rather easier.

Decide framework

Once the information has been collected and objectives thought out, the framework of the course can be worked out. Jean Rudduck[48] makes the following points about successful courses:

1 Course members respond well to a course which demonstrates that the course leader has put a lot of effort into its preparation. The evidence for sound preparation includes appropriate handouts, overhead projector transparencies, lecture notes and resources for discussion.
2 Course members respond well to a course where the content is thoroughly researched and professionally presented.
3 Course members respond well to sessions which are varied in rhythm and have a range of activity; this seems particularly important when teachers come, rather tired, straight from a full working day in school.
4 Course members respond well to lectures – if lectures are the appropriate medium – which are lively and provocative and which generate confidence in the speaker.
5 Course members respond well to advisers' attempts to build in opportunities for discussion – even though they acknowledge that as participants they do not always make the most of these opportunities.
6 Course members respond well to attempts to test theory by reference to practice, preferably if the practice can be illustrated from their own classrooms.

Consider/prepare

Decisions are needed about activities, speakers, a time plan, grouping, a space plan, resources and handouts.

Activities

A wide range of activities is listed on pp. 92–101, which should enable anyone planning a course to provide a suitable variety. It is important to remember that a basic element in the learning process is the need to make learning one's own by talking about it or working with what has been learned. This is as true for teachers as it is for pupils.

Discussion is particularly important but is frequently an unsatisfactory part of a course. There are several reasons for this:

1 The discussion brief is not sufficiently clearly defined. Course organizers need to consider the function of the discussion and what it is intended should come out of it.
2 The group is too large. About eight is large enough if people are really going to contribute and learn. It can be rather larger where people already know one another well.
3 The leadership is inadequate. Leading discussion is an important skill which teachers have not necessarily developed by being in a senior post. Suggestions for training discussion leaders are given in the list of activities below.

Speakers

If you decide to have speakers from outside the school, or even from inside, you need to plan a long time in advance because diaries fill up; good speakers are unlikely to be able to come if approached too near the date you want them.

It is helpful to give speakers as much information as you can. They need to know the overall aims of your professional development programme and of the particular part of it to which you are inviting them to contribute. Speakers should be given a clear brief for their talk so that what they offer really fits in with what is happening during the course. They should be asked what they need by way of resources and materials and what they may be bringing and what they are expecting the school to provide. Arrangements about a fee and expenses should also be given in the letter of invitation; you should ask whether overnight accommodation will be required. All this information should be sent out when the speaker is invited.

It is important to keep the initiative in arranging overnight accommodation. Some hotels are now very expensive and someone making his or her own booking from a distance may quite inadvertantly exceed the budget. It may also be necessary to book up a long time in advance in some areas of the country.

If the speaker accepts the invitation a letter should be sent within about three weeks of the date of the course, giving the course programme as it has been given to course participants together with information about the course venue and how to get there, offering to meet a train if necessary. It should also contain information about the accommodation which has been arranged.

Arrangements for paying speakers should be sorted out well in advance of the course so that expense claim forms (if any) can be given out and payment can follow quickly.

Time plan

Some decisions about timing will have been taken in planning the school programme but it may be possible to decide the length of sessions and it will certainly be possible to decide the way that time is to be allocated during the period the course is run.

Much that we know about dealing with children also applies with adults. Any concentrated input should be near the beginning of the course; it is as well to remember that although people who are really interested can concentrate on a speaker for a long time, most people concentrate well for only about twenty minutes. This suggests that a series of short inputs with practical work in between is better than a long speech, although when an outside speaker is invited short inputs are not really a possibility. A good deal of the time at any course should involve people working together in small groups and should draw on the skills and knowledge of the course participants.

People also have high and low points during the day: these should be taken into account in making the time plan. They are usually most receptive first thing in the morning and attention wanes as the day wears on. The periods after meals are usually low points and participants need to be involved in an interesting activity at this stage. In a residential course the period after dinner needs careful planning. This is often a good time for films or videos, or for leadership games which involve everyone and are fun.

Grouping

Some part of the course may require work in groups. If the composition of the groups is unimportant then people can be simply asked to get into groups of whatever number is needed. For a number of purposes within a staff, however, it may be better to place people in groups so that they meet people whom they normally see little of. This can be done simply by arranging the groups or by an activity which places people in groups. For example everyone can be given a number and all those with, say, the number 4 make one group.

It is also sometimes wise within a staff to separate out those who are fairly negative in their views and place them in different groups and likewise to spread those who have positive views.

A further reason for special groups within a staff is that very junior staff may well be intimidated if they find themselves in a group with the most senior members of the staff or the headteacher and may not contribute as a result.

Space plan

Most courses involve different activities which require different arrangements of furniture. It is as well to consider this in advance. It may be possible to arrange one room so that different parts of it can be used for different activities in which case it will need arranging carefully in advance of the course. On the other hand it may be necessary to decide whether the furniture in one room needs to be rearranged or whether it is easier to have different arrangements of furniture in adjacent rooms if they are available. If a rearrangement of the furniture is needed it is as well to plan this in advance so that the change occurs smoothly.

Where furniture is being arranged for a lecture, it is important to check sight lines, particularly if audio-visual equipment is to be used. It is also wise to check for sound problems in order to decide whether a microphone is needed.

Group discussion needs chairs in circles. Where discussion takes place with some chairs in a row, the people in the row are unlikely to discuss with one another, because they cannot see everyone.

Resources

The importance of planning ahead for resources was noted earlier in this chapter. Materials should be assembled early enough to be sure that everything needed is available. It is also important to consider whether there are items which course members might be expected to bring with them, but it is unwise to rely too heavily on this. There is always someone who forgets something and spare items are needed to provide for this. It is also wise to have spare projector bulbs (and to know how to change the bulb if necessary).

On the day of the course, equipment should be checked in position and, where appropriate, focused ready for use. Materials should be checked over and set out ready for use.

Projectors should be checked for focus just before the course starts.

Handouts

Handouts may be sent out as preliminary reading or distributed at some stage during the course. Thought should be given to the function of handouts. Those sent out before a course may be intended to get everyone to a certain point of understanding ready for the course, although one cannot rely on participants actually reading the papers. Handouts used during the course may be a summary of a talk given or complementary to the work done or a mixture of both. The purpose of the handout may decide when during the course it is distributed. If it is a summary of the content then there is much to be said for giving it out at the beginning so that participants can make notes which are complementary to the handout rather than making notes on the whole lecture. If it is complementary then it seems more sensible to give it out at the end of the meeting so that people have something to take away with them.

One of the findings of Jean Rudduck[48] was that the handout most appreciated by teachers was the booklist.

Cost course

Two kinds of costing of programmes are needed – costing of time and costing in money.

Travel

This will be necessary only when the activity is held away from the school, but as local financial management develops schools are likely to have to pay travel for many of the courses and meetings which teachers attend. This will need estimating on an annual basis and the school will need to keep a fairly close check on how much is being spent. The travel costs of courses tend to add up to a considerable sum.

Accommodation

This, like travel, will be necessary only for courses held away from the school, but it will include the costs of accommodation for external courses attended by members of staff.

Food

Almost all courses and conference involve food costs, even if it is only the cost of a cup of tea. This will include not only the cost of the materials, but also the cost of those preparing and serving them. If teachers provide the food, their time needs to be considered.

Materials

Most courses involve using some materials such as paper, OHP transparencies, video tapes, films, etc. While some materials are very cheap, the cost of hiring tapes can be very high indeed.

Speakers and leaders

This is a very confused area. There are some speakers, such as LEA advisers and HMI, who will give their services free. Other people may charge a very wide range of sums, depending on how well known and how busy they are. It is very important to try to get this worked out well in advance. Speakers can also cost a good deal in expenses if they come from a distance; it is important to establish a mileage rate well in advance and to select a hotel you can afford for any overnight stay.

Supply cover

This is much the most expensive part of the course programme and needs very careful consideration, especially as a supply teacher does not truly cover for the teacher who is elsewhere (even if one can be obtained). The ideal is for the school to have a small group of supply teachers who know the school and the pupils and fit in easily, but this is unrealistic in some areas.

Evaluation and follow-up

It is important to plan evaluation at the same time as the rest of the course because there will be costs involved, including both time and money, which have to be budgeted for. The costs of evaluation range from the cost of paper and copying of questionnaires to the cost of an external evaluator or the cost in time of an internal evaluator. A first reaction may be that it is not possible to consider paying an external evaluator, but if using an internal evaluator involves freeing the person concerned by using supply cover, this could be just as expensive.

Follow-up may also require resources if the tutors of a course visit the teachers who attended during working hours in their classrooms.

Send out information

Once everything is planned information about the course can be sent out. The timing of this is important. If information is sent out too early, people may forget about the course. If it is too late diaries will be full and people will not come. The best solution is to send out an early preliminary notice a long time in advance and then send out the details about six weeks from the course itself. The information sent out should give a full account of the objectives of the course and details of how these objectives are to be met. Anyone coming to a course should have as clear an idea as possible of what will happen. Most people are irritated if a course turns out to be different from what they expected.

The actual title given to the course and the way it is described is important. Teachers tend to be put off where the course title and information suggest a very theoretical approach.

Evaluate

Every course should have some evaluation built into it. This may take a variety of forms, which are discussed in Chapter 13.

At this stage it is important to do two things. First, plans for the course should be checked over, looking at the following questions.

1 Does what is planned seem likely to meet the stated objectives?
2 Does what is planned make a coherent whole with logical relationships between the different parts of the course?
3 Does the time plan take into account the normal attention span and provide suitable activities for the low points in the day, such as after meals and the end of the day?
4 Are the approaches planned sufficiently varied to maintain the interest of the participants?
5 Do plans include sufficient involvement of the participants?
6 Does what is planned allow participants to build on their own experience?
7 Is what is planned sufficiently linked to the participants' normal work to make it easy for them to see its relevance and use what is being learned?

Second, evaluation of the course needs planning at the preliminary stage so that any information needed for evaluation can be collected. Planned evaluation also helps to ensure that it actually takes place and that it is someone's responsibility to undertake it.

Arrange follow-up activities

In-service activity is useful only if it leads to more effective work in the classroom. Each training event needs to be designed with this in mind and most training sessions should end with the teachers concerned making action plans which are then followed up by the course leaders.

Jean Rudduck[48] differentiates between **follow-up**, as activity by the course leaders, and **follow-through**, as activity by the teachers. She divides follow-through into implementation, which is the ability of the teacher to apply in the classroom the skills and knowledge acquired on the course, and development, which is the teacher's ability to build on from what he or she has learned. Both require consideration as part of the course and teachers need to consider what obstacles they are likely to encounter in trying to put new thinking into practice. This is likely to be rather less in the context of school-based and focused work than in an external course. When everyone on the course is from the same school, the problems of implementation will be shared and can be tackled more easily.

However well the matter of follow-through is tackled during the course, there is still a need to follow-up in some way. Ideally the course tutor should visit everyone in the classroom to talk over the problems which are emerging and ways of tackling them. This may be difficult to do because of the time involved and it may be easier to arrange a meeting of everyone who was at the course at a later stage so that problems can be discussed. A questionnaire, sent out some time after the course, may identify particular problems which can be tackled by visiting or a meeting: it may be possible to put people having difficulty in touch with others who seem to be succeeding. Pairing is useful anyway and teachers can pair off at the course with the object of comparing notes about how they get on with implementing what they have learned.

Course activities

The list which follows gives a number of possible activities which can be used as part of in-service activity.

Action learning

Action learning was originally devised by R. W. Revans and is described in *Action Learning*.[51] It involves a group of people working together to study problems in each of their working contexts. The group, called a learning 'set', has a 'set adviser' who acts as a facilitator. It does not necessarily have to be a group of people with similar work; it might well be a group of teachers from different schools.

The set provides opportunities for each person to analyse his or her problems with support from the set, who also help in devising strategies for tackling the problems. Between meetings the members work on their problems and bring their findings back to the set. Eventually the set evaluates what has happened as a result of their work and this may lead to further work. See also Pedlar.[52]

Active listening

The ability to listen is required in many aspects of a teacher's work and particularly for those in management roles who will be involved in appraisal. Teachers are more used to talking than listening and consideration of what is involved in the process of listening can be valuable.

In this activity, teachers are asked to work in pairs. Each person in turn is asked to be the listener, while the other talks about some aspect of his or her work or some other topic of interest for about three minutes, carefully timed. The pairs are then asked to consider whether the speaker felt that the listener was listening and what clues there were to suggest this. This should lead to the identification of the way people behave when they are listening intently.

A further development of this activity is to use it as an ice-breaker at the beginning of a course. Each person talks about his or her job. After discussion about what is involved in listening the pairs join up in fours and each person describes to the group what is involved in his or her partner's job.

Assertiveness training

Assertiveness is the ability to stand up for one's own ideas and rights in a way which does not diminish others or violate their rights. Assertiveness training involves learning verbal and non-verbal behaviour which enables a person to be assertive rather than aggressive or passive, that is failing to express needs, wants or opinions or to stand up for rights. Training involves some explanation of assertiveness and some exploration of the kinds of situations in which assertive behaviour may be required. It also involves role-play of situations which could involve aggressive behaviour, non-assertive behaviour or assertive behaviour and considering how to be assertive in each.

Ideas about activities which could be used to train assertive behaviour may be found in *Assertiveness at Work* by Ken and Kate Back.[53]

Brainstorming

Brainstorming is a valuable way of exploring thinking and of collecting ideas. It is best undertaken in small groups of about eight or fewer. If the group is larger there is not the same pressure on group members to produce ideas. There should be a group leader. Members are asked for all the ideas they can think of about a particular topic, no matter whether the ideas are sensible or unlikely. These are all listed on a flip chart or OHP. The group leader presses people for ideas and is welcoming to every idea put forward.

When a certain number of ideas have been collected or a certain time has elapsed, the list is considered and the possible ideas are selected out from the unlikely ones. The group may then vote for one particular idea to use or explore the possibilities of a number of ideas. (See ideas collection, p. 96, and nominal group technique, p. 98.) One useful way of exploring the ideas further is to take each idea in turn and think of all the good reasons there are for using it. This may be followed by a consideration of all the problems likely to be involved in using a particular idea. Or each idea can be taken in turn and pros, cons and points of interest can be noted.

Broadcast material

The BBC in particular makes many programmes for teachers which are worth using as discussion material for a group. Lists of these are found in BBC catalogues. It is important that the person leading this kind of discussion has seen or heard the material in advance and has prepared some lines of discussion so that what follows is profitable. This also makes it possible to suggest that those watching look out for particular points.

Buzz groups

One way of improving the follow-up to a lecture is to ask the participants to discuss it in groups of three without moving significantly from their seats. This can lead to a much better absorption of the lecture material and to better questioning of the lecturer when the plenary session is recalled.

Case studies

Case study material can easily be provided by any school or teacher and a small group of teachers can sit down together to discuss what is involved and the alternative approaches which might be tried. The material can be from classrooms, looking at the problems posed by particular pupils or it can be a management problem, looking at difficulties in a particular area of work.

See also S. Goulding *et al.*[54] and A. Paisey.[55]

Critical incident analysis

Critical incidents are those which are seen to give rise to problems. One way of tackling the problems is to collect information about critical incidents and try to analyse how and why they occur. For example one group of teachers collected information about the occasions when individual pupils created indiscipline in the classroom, noting the time and the situation. This enabled them to discover some of the points which the critical incidents had in common and start to undertake problem-solving activities.

Delphi

Delphi is a useful way of collecting information about how people view things, which helps a group to home in on the areas in which they think differently.

It requires a series of statements about the topic under consideration with space for grading each statement (as in Figure 6). Each member of the group is then asked to complete a sheet of statements, grading each one. The collection of statements is then entered on a single sheet by putting a number for the number of ticks in each column. This is best put on an OHP transparency so that everyone can see it. It is then used as material for discussion, concentrating particularly on those items where people thought very differently. This kind of

Figure 6   Delphi

DELPHI	++	+	av	−	− −
Teachers develop their work best through their experience in the classroom					
The most useful way of developing one's work is to work on something with another person					

exercise may actually change the attitudes of some people. It will also give the course organizers information about how people see things.

Discussion leadership

The importance of good leadership for discussion was noted earlier. One way of training this skill is to set up a discussion with a chosen leader and one or more observers, whose task is to observe what the leader is doing. A good leader should respond positively to contributions from course members, perhaps by making comments like 'that's a good idea' or 'that's helpful', or weaving them into the work of the group by relating them to other contributions. The group should be scanned from time to time to see whether any individual wishes to contribute. As the discussion proceeds the leader needs to sum up so that the group can see where they have reached and a full summing up should come at the end.

Discussion leadership may be trained by having observers watching a particular discussion leader at work. The observer may record what happens in terms of the activity of the leader and the group, or may study some aspect of the activity such as body language, with a view to making everyone conscious of the way a group leader must read the body language of the group. Alternatively the observer may record the interactions using a diagram such as Figure 7, in which the letters stand for the group members. The lines across are the exchanges between members with the arrows showing the direction of the exchange. The strokes across the arrows show the number of exchanges and the strokes outside the circle show the statements made to the whole group.

Figure 7   Discussion leadership

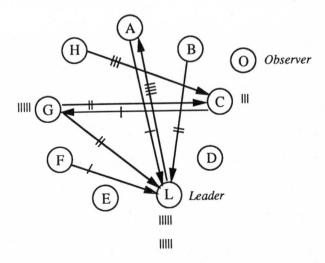

This kind of diagram gives a picture of the pattern of discussion and the extent to which it is dominated by the group leader. We should expect to find the group leader making a number of comments to the whole group but not too many. It will also show those who are not joining in.

Further suggestions and details of ways of recording and training discussion group leaders can be found in *Leading Discussion*,[56] *Managing the Primary School*[28] and *Managing the Secondary School*.[29]

Group problem-solving

There are a number of techniques for problem-solving which can be used in groups. A problem-solving group needs a good leader who has the skills required for discussion leadership described above. The task is then one of defining the problem clearly, brainstorming possible alternatives, selecting appropriate solutions and developing them. It is a good idea to plan for a later evaluation of how well the solution chosen worked in practice.

Goldfish bowl activities

This refers to all the activities which can be carried out using observers, such as those suggested under discussion leadership and problem-solving interviewing. The process can also be used for considering how meetings are conducted, with a group undertaking one of its normal meetings or a simulated meeting watched by observers who give feedback on the effectiveness of the meeting.

Ideas collection

Ideas about a number of topics may be collected by circulating a number of overhead projection transparencies on each of which every person in the group writes an idea. This is useful when, for example, a number of aims or objectives have been stated and the group is looking for ways of meeting them. An aim or objective can be stated at the top of each sheet and each person adds an idea about how to achieve it as the sheets are passed round.

When the group feels that enough ideas have been collected, each sheet can be projected and the ideas on it considered in one of the ways described under brainstorming.

Information circuit

The situation sometimes occurs where there are several people who have information to give to the whole group. The usual way of dealing with this is let them each have a short period to speak to the group. The trouble with this is that it can be somewhat intense for the listeners, who may cease to take anything in by the time the last speaker is reached.

A different approach to this is to form as many groups as there are speakers and ask each group to think of questions they would like to pursue with the speakers. Each speaker then has a short period with each group which allows for discussion of the information and speakers move from group to group at specified intervals. This activity can go on for longer than a series of talks because of the involvement of the groups. Ideally each speaker should have about half-an-hour with each group. From the speakers' point of view this has the advantage that all the preparation is done by the groups. From the organizer's point of view the advantage is that much more is gained from the speakers, who are giving all the time they are there.

Information exchange

It is often profitable for course participants to spend some time discussing how they each do a particular thing. It is helpful to ask members to bring with them information about the topic under discussion which can be given to two other members. The whole group can be asked to work in threes and to exchange the information they have brought. This can be a particularly useful way of starting a session when people do not all arrive at the same time, because threes can be formed for discussion as soon as there are enough people.

In-tray activities

This is a popular management training activity in which a group is asked to consider the papers facing someone at a particular management level and to decide how they should be dealt with. This is valuable for those who are in management roles, but it is helpful to those who are aspiring to leadership to consider the problems involved.

Making a presentation

Although the formal lecture is not always a very effective way of learning it becomes so when those listening are well prepared for it and are wanting to hear the kinds of things the lecturer has to offer. Other forms of presentation which may provide opportunities for valuable discussion include video recordings, films, tape/slide sequences, computer programs and many variations of these.

Preparing a presentation to colleagues in an area of work in which a teacher is expert can be a very valuable form of professional development for the person concerned.

The value of this exercise can be increased if, after the presentation, there is consideration about what was good about it and what might have been improved. This consideration should involve use of voice and gesture, the structure of the talk and ability to hold the audience, the use of visual aids and any habits which interfered with listening. Further information about making a presentation together with a form for assessing competence, can be found in *Talking to a Group*.[57]

Micro-teaching

This is a technique often used in initial training to give students the opportunity to practise one particular detailed aspect of the teacher's task by reducing all the other aspects. The student thus deals with a small number of pupils for a short time and has a clear brief about what is to be done in that time. Normally one student teaches a small group while others observe. The exercise is then followed by discussion. It could be used as part of the training of probationers and also to some extent with experienced teachers to develop new techniques. Work on questioning, for example, would lend itself to this. It might also be helpful in considering how to react to various kinds of indiscipline in the classroom.

Nominal group technique

This is a useful way of getting expressions of opinion from a group which really involves all members. It is particularly useful for evaluating activities.

Each member of the group is asked to write down as many points as he or she can about the matter in question. These can be listed in groups of points, perhaps listing positive and negative points separately. When everyone has completed his or her lists all the lists about each aspect are combined by going round the group, collecting points and writing them on a flip chart until no more remain. Everyone then votes for an agreed number of points – perhaps six or ten – and this gives the overall views of the group.

Problem-solving interviews

Most people in management roles find themselves interviewing people about problems. This can be explored by working in threes, with one person acting as interviewer, one as interviewee and one as observer. The interviewee should select an actual problem in his or her daily life which is not yet solved and in which help would be welcome. The task of the interviewer is to find out about the problem and help the interviewee to find some solutions. The problems must be genuine so that they have all the detail which may be needed in the discussion. Both interviewer and interviewee are playing themselves. In attempting to help the interviewee, the interviewer should try to lead the other person to his or her own solutions, suggesting solutions only as ideas to select from. It is important to avoid saying in effect 'This is how you should deal with this situation', since different people have different ways of tackling problems and the task is to help the interviewee find one which suits him or her.

A strict time limit should be given for each part of the exercise. About thirty minutes for the problem discussion, followed by about fifteen minutes for discussion about what happened is usually satisfactory.

When the time limit has been reached the observer gives feedback on the way the interview went and the skills that were used and draws the interviewee into the discussion to give the interviewer feedback on how the interviewing felt on the receiving end.

A variation on this is to ask people, while still playing themselves, to assume that one or other of them is the senior. The effect of this in both directions is valuable to discuss, particularly for headteachers and senior managers in schools.

This exercise can also be used to practise appraisal interviewing or counselling or any other activity in which two people have a discussion in a one-to-one situation. In some situations, appraisal interviewing, for example, there will need to be a measure of role-play. For further information see *Interviewing*.[58]

Quality circles

A quality circle is a small group of volunteers with work in common which meets regularly to identify, analyse and solve work problems. The group should be between four and ten members. Its members may need training in problem-solving skills and in working together as a group. See Robson.[59]

Role-play

Role-play is a useful device for learning in a number of areas. It is useful for appraisal interviewing, selection interviewing exercises and for a meeting as a goldfish bowl activity. There are some problems involved in its use. Adults are sometime unwilling to play parts and embarrassed at what is being asked of them. Most people overcome this fairly quickly when they get into the task in hand. There is also the problem of giving too much or too little information about the participants. It is generally best to give a fairly brief account and suggest that the participants invent what is not there. The most difficult problem is that someone playing the part of a difficult character can go on being difficult to a far greater extent than is common in real life. This may provide an interesting opportunity for everyone to discuss different ways of tackling such a problem and then to replay the activity.

Self-development

Self-development may be part of the process of appraisal within the school or it may be something undertaken with individuals or it can be part of a training programme. It will involve helping individuals to see themselves from various points of view and may use one of a number of activities devised to help this.

Figure 8   Johari's window

	Known to self	Unknown to self
Known to others	**1** **OPEN**	**2** **BLIND**
Unknown to others	**3** **HIDDEN**	**4** **CLOSED**

For example Johari's window (Figure 8) is often used as a starting-point for discussion and work. Other people may help an individual to know what is in quadrant 2. The aim is to enlarge what is in 1 and to reduce what is in 2, 3 and 4. See Francis and Woodcock.[60]

Team building

Good management involves work in teams. If people are to work together as a team there must be openness and trust between them, a clear sense of direction and sound leadership. Team-building activities generally consist of activities designed to help groups to reflect upon the work of the teams they are in, to increase openness and trust and activities in small teams which can be observed and analysed. A large number of such activities are described in detail by Mike Woodcock.[61]

One activity designed to help groups to reflect on the teams they are in involves pairs of groups which normally work together. Each group goes to a separate room and prepares on a flip chart sheet:

1 a list of adjectives describing the other group
2 a list of adjectives describing themselves.

Each group then displays the two lists and the differences are discussed, looking at the positive and negative adjectives.

One way of exploring the issue of openness is by asking people to answer the following questions for each member of the group. This also has relevance for the self-development described above.

1 The things I have found most valuable about you are . . .
2 Your major strengths are . . .
3 Your most helpful actions in our group have been . . .
4 Your principal weaknesses in the group are . . .
5 The types of behaviour you should try to change are . . .

The answers are then discussed. Alternatively each person can be given the answers relating to him or her from each other member of the group.

This kind of activity is clearly sensitive but its use might increase the appreciation of members for each other. If it is felt that this kind of activity is going too far, it would be possible to take the positive questions only and work on those initially.

Team work can be studied using almost any team task. It is possible to take an actual task such as planning an activity or to use something remote from normal work like a game of some kind or an attempt to make or build something which requires team work. In each case observers are needed who look at such issues as those described in the *Team Development Manual*.[61]

1 What actions helped the group to accomplish the task?
2 Which actions hindered the group in completing the task?
3 How did leadership emerge in the team?
4 Who participated most?
5 Who participated least?
6 What feelings did members experience as the task progressed?
7 What suggestions could be made to improve team performance?

7

The role of management in professional development

Professional development is a whole-school activity. Everyone in a management role in a school therefore has responsibility for developing the work of the teachers for whom he or she is responsible. In the case of the small primary school, the responsibility is normally that of the headteacher, with some help from the deputy. In a larger primary school it may be shared with the deputy and with heads of year or curriculum co-ordinators. In a secondary school it is widely shared, with a part played by the deputies, the heads of faculty, department and year and possibly some others.

In addition it has now become common practice to appoint someone to take responsibility overall for staff development. This is a key role for co-ordinating what is happening, but not a substitute for professional development work by other managers. It is important that the boundaries between the roles are clearly drawn.

The role of senior management

In order to see clearly what the role of the professional development co-ordinator might be, the role of the headteacher (and in secondary schools, the senior management team) must be considered. This might be summarised as follows:

1 Articulate aims and policies for the school, following consultation and discussion and communicate them to everyone concerned.
2 Articulate the curriculum philosophy of the school, following consultation and discussion and make it explicit for staff, pupils, governors and the community.

3 Organize the school effectively for teaching and learning.
4 Establish a philosophy and a structure for care and discipline in consultation within everyone concerned.
5 Oversee the administrative work of the school and control the school finances.
6 Maintain appropriate external relationships.
7 Evaluate the work of the school in all its aspects.
8 Establish and maintain a school policy for professional development, including an appraisal programme.

Establishing a school policy for professional development

This task involves

1 setting priorities, including ensuring that the school meets the requirements of national and LEA policies
2 creating a structure for professional development
3 selecting and appointing staff for professional development tasks
4 clarifying professional development roles
5 co-ordinating professional development policy with other school policies
6 allocating resources for professional development
7 creating an organization for appraisal.

These tasks can be looked at in more detail.

Setting priorities, including ensuring that the school meets the requirements of national and LEA policies

There is at present much in-service work needed to enable teachers to adapt to the changes which are happening in education. It is the task of the headteacher and senior management to see that this training takes place. This may be at the expense of other training which teachers would prefer.

Creating a structure for professional development

The headteacher and senior management must see that there is an adequate organization for in-service work. This may be a committee; in a small primary school it may involve the whole staff.

Selecting and appointing staff for professional development tasks

In practice headteachers are not usually in a position to select staff freely for these roles, because they rarely have the opportunity to create completely new posts. More usually the task is one of considering existing staff and trying to decide which person or persons might be able to take on what is involved in addition to their current responsibilities. It is important that whoever takes on the role of professional development co-ordinator has sufficient seniority and sufficient delegated authority as well as the skills and personality to do the job.

Clarifying professional development roles

It is important to spell out the professional development responsibilities for the co-ordinator and for those in other management roles and to make sure that all staff are aware of how responsibilities are held.

Co-ordinating professional development policy with other school policies

The policy and programme for professional development should reflect the school policies in some sense.

Allocating resources for professional development

This means seeing that time has been allowed for planning and organizing in-service work as well as for actually taking part in it. It also means assessing how much supply cover can be allowed and how much money can be used for professional development purposes.

Creating an organization for appraisal

Details of possible ways of organizing appraisal are given in Chapter 8.

The role of middle management

In secondary schools and the larger primary schools there will be others in management roles who have a professional development responsibility for a small group of colleagues. In a small primary school, these responsibilities will fall upon the headteacher and deputy.

Responsibilities

These responsibilities might involve

1 observing each colleague at work and discussing what happened
2 providing opportunities for colleagues to observe each other at work and exchange information about the way they do things
3 discussing work with individuals, identifying their professional development needs, providing for some of them and informing the professional development co-ordinator of others

4 providing group opportunities for discussing work
5 involving colleagues in planning and decision-making, including some of the preceding research
6 providing colleagues with opportunities to undertake leadership tasks from time to time
7 providing opportunities for colleagues to learn what is involved in the management post in question
8 ensuring that colleagues keep up-to-date in the area of work with which they are concerned and in education more generally
9 seeing that the professional development needs of the group are known and provided for either at school level, or through external provision.

These responsibilities will now be considered in more detail.

Observing each colleague at work and discussing what happened

This will be a necessary part of the preparation for appraisal and should be seen as a normal part of the work of anyone in a management role. It should be stressed that the idea is to provide advice which will be helpful for development. This is discussed further in Chapter 8.

Providing opportunities for colleagues to observe each other at work and exchange information about the way they do things

Teachers need models from which they can develop their own teaching style, particularly at the beginning of their careers. Teachers who do not have the opportunity to see a range of teaching models will fall back on the models they know best – those offered by the teachers who taught them in childhood. These may not be good models and it is therefore very important that inexperienced teachers, in particular, see good models of teaching. Experienced teachers too can gain from seeing how others do things and exchanging information. It is very difficult for teachers to arrange such opportunities for themselves. It is therefore an important responsibility for those in management roles.

Discussing work with individuals, identifying their professional development needs, providing for some of them and informing the professional development co-ordinator of others

The middle management in a large school has an important role to play in ensuring that the work on needs assessment properly reflects teachers' needs. Some of this information will emerge as part of the appraisal process and some as part of discussion about work. The important thing is that the middle manager concerned should be aware of his or her responsibilities for assessing and where possible meeting the needs of colleagues.

Providing group opportunities for discussing work

Most teachers learn a great deal from discussing their work with colleagues. Opportunities need to be made for doing this, however. Departmental and year meetings can be simply business meetings with little discussion about the work itself. Issues like stating aims and objectives, discussing teaching approaches, and identifying criteria for selecting materials have considerable development possibilities.

Involving colleagues in planning and decision-making,
including some of the preceding research

The opportunity to take part in decision-making is valuable for development. Many decisions require prior research to collect relevant information and this too can be shared so that people learn from the activity.

Providing colleagues with opportunities to undertake leadership
tasks from time to time

One of the best kinds of preparation for a management role is to have the opportunity to lead a small group. There can be many opportunities for this. A teacher who has attended a useful course outside the school may lead a group session in which others are informed about the course. A group member may have done some research in order to contribute to group decision-making and may take the lead in discussing this. Different members of the group may lead discussion, perhaps with some feedback on their success in the role of discussion leader.

Providing opportunities for colleagues to learn what is involved
in the management post in question

Delegation of different aspects of a management role from time to time offers valuable preparation of others for that role. This has to be done diplomatically and must be clearly seen as development.

Ensuring that colleagues keep up-to-date in the area of work with
which they are concerned and in education more generally

Education is moving very fast in all areas of work and it is not easy to keep up-to-date. It is the responsibility of those in management roles to see that their colleagues are informed about what is happening. This may be done by sharing out areas to pursue within the group and then sharing the information, by identifying particular courses and seminars at which the group should be represented or by planning a reading programme with a sharing of information.

Seeing that the professional development needs of the group are known and provided for either at school level, or through external provision

The middle manager must see the development needs of colleagues as his or her responsibility. They should be known and provision for them pursued both within the school and externally.

The professional development co-ordinator

The key person so far as professional development is concerned is the professional development co-ordinator. Oldroyd and Hall[27] note that people in this role may have a variety of titles, e.g. INSET Co-ordinator, Deputy Head (Staff Development), Staff Development Officer, Staff Development Co-ordinator or Professional Tutor. The inclusion of the deputy head title makes it clear that the status of the post is important whatever it is called. The person undertaking it must be part of the senior management structure or at least have formal opportunities for working with the senior management of the school. The status of the post is important because the person concerned will be responsible for some decisions which cannot, by their nature, please everyone. At the same time it is important that the person chosen for this post has very good interpersonal skills, because he or she will need to proceed by persuasion on many occasions.

Responsibilities

The professional development co-ordinator's responsibilities will depend on the size of the school and the way it is organized. Many of them will be supported by the work of the professional development committee. These responsibilities might involve

1 co-ordinating the professional development programme for the school
2 providing leadership for the professional development committee
3 co-ordinating the assessment of the professional development needs of the staff and the analysis of findings
4 drawing up the professional development programme and ensuring that everyone is aware of what it contains
5 co-ordinating the evaluation of the professional development programme and of individual units within it and communicating the results to those concerned
6 providing advice, support and training for colleagues contributing to the school professional development programme
7 keeping in touch with those providing INSET outside the school and advising colleagues on appropriate courses for their needs

8 ensuring that all staff are kept fully aware of professional development opportunities available to them
9 providing advice and support for colleagues concerned about their professional development needs
10 keeping the senior management and other staff aware of the learning opportunities available as part of the daily life of the school.

These responsibilities can be looked at in further detail.

Co-ordinating the professional development programme for the school

The professional development co-ordinator, as leader of the development committee, has overall responsibility for the programme. He or she should see that it fits the needs of the school and of individuals as far as possible and should see it as a long-term programme which is partly implemented year by year.

Providing leadership for the professional development committee

Leadership involves more than chairing a committee. It involves helping the committee to work as a team, drawing from each member what he or she has to give. It involves not only suggesting ideas, but also making it possible for others to come up with ideas. It involves helping the committee to see the direction in which they are going, summing up their thinking, identifying clear aims and objectives, working towards them, and modifying them if this seems appropriate in the light of new demands.

Co-ordinating the assessment of the professional development needs of the staff and the analysis of findings

The committee may decide how to assess the needs of the staff and the school, but it is the co-ordinator's responsibility to analyse the findings and make them available to the committee. Others in management roles may come to him or her to talk about the development needs of colleagues; in a primary school where this organization does not exist it may also be necessary for the co-ordinator to interview each member of staff about his or her needs. There is also a case for some discussion with the headteacher about the needs of teachers of which the teachers themselves are not aware.

Drawing up the professional development programme and ensuring that everyone is aware of what it contains

It is the co-ordinator's responsibility to put the programme into writing in the light of discussion in the committee and to see that it is made public and that everyone is aware of it.

*Co-ordinating the evaluation of the professional development
programme and of individual units within it and
communicating results to those concerned*

The co-ordinator should see that each part of the programme is evaluated effectively and that the information is fed back to those responsible. He or she should draw together all the evaluation reports for the committee to consider so that they can be taken into account in planning the following year's programme.

*Providing advice, support and training for colleagues
contributing to the school professional development programme*

As schools take greater responsibility for their own staff development programme, it is likely that more of the programme will be run by teachers within the school. These teachers will need training in the skills involved. (This is dealt with in greater detail on pp. 113–15.) The co-ordinator must be responsible for the training programme and for advising those who take on training roles.

*Keeping in touch with those providing INSET outside the school
and advising colleagues on appropriate courses for their needs*

The co-ordinator should have a full picture of what is happening in the LEA, in the local teachers' centres and in local institutions of higher education. He or she should have a strong link with whoever is in the co-ordinating role in the LEA and should have available information about what is happening nationally. The co-ordinator should be able to advise colleagues in full knowledge of what is available locally and should keep the committee informed.

*Ensuring that all staff are kept fully aware of professional
development opportunities available to them*

The co-ordinator has an important role as a communicator and it is his or her responsibility to see that all teachers are aware of what is within the school programme and what is available externally. The co-ordinator should also keep the headteacher and senior management informed.

*Providing advice and support for colleagues concerned about
their professional development needs*

The co-ordinator should be the person whom teachers turn to when they want to discuss their future development and their training needs. He or she should be in a position to give valid career advice as well as information about courses and learning opportunities within the school.

Keeping senior management and other staff aware of the
learning opportunities available as part of the daily life of
the school

We have seen earlier that there are many opportunities for development within the school, of which people are often unaware. It is the responsibility of the co-ordinator to see that everyone recognizes and uses these opportunities.

Personal qualities

Ideally the co-ordinator of professional development needs to be a person who makes good relationships easily, is tactful and diplomatic, sympathetic with colleagues but clear sighted about their needs. Enthusiasm is needed together with a considerable capacity for hard work.

Skills

The co-ordinator of professional development will also need a particular range of skills and knowledge in the following areas:

1 making relationships
2 leading thinking
3 counselling and guiding
4 active listening
5 negotiating
6 planning
7 organizing
8 chairing a group
9 evaluating

A headteacher will be fortunate if there is on the staff someone with all these skills who is able to undertake this work. It is more likely that there will be someone who has some of what is needed who can be encouraged to learn in other areas. For example someone who gets on well with others, and who has ability to lead thinking, may be able to learn how to undertake needs assessment and evaluation and develop skill in the counselling role. Thought must be given therefore to the professional development needs of the co-ordinator, if he or she is to function effectively. Suggestions for training some of the necessary skills are given below. These complement the suggestions already given in Chapter 6.

Making relationships

The most important of the skills needed by the co-ordinator, without which other skills may be difficult to use, is the ability to make good relationships with other people and lead their thinking.

To a large extent the ability to make relationships is something individuals acquire in the process of growing up. People can improve this skill with training, however, and the suggestions put forward under 'assertiveness training' (p. 93) and under 'team building' (p. 100) and 'self-development' (pp. 99–100) will be useful. It is very difficult to change someone who is bad at making relationships into someone good at it, but training can make a difference.

Leading thinking

There is considerable skill involved in helping the thinking of a group to move forward. It is not a matter of doing the thinking for them but one of drawing ideas from them and seeking ways of putting the ideas together and using them to move forward. It is a skill most easily practised in the context of group discussion and the suggestions for training 'discussion leadership' (pp. 95–6) provide a good way of training the ability to lead thinking.

Counselling and guiding

Skill in counselling involves active listening and the ability to help another person sort out his or her thinking by using different forms of questioning and response. The skill is to help people to formulate their own ideas rather than to impose ideas upon them, but to lead them by what is selected for comment and by questioning. Suggestions for methods of training counselling were given under 'problem-solving interviews' (pp. 98–9). There are also relevant suggestions in Chapter 10, which considers the appraisal interview.

Active listening

The ability to listen is a very important skill for the co-ordinator. Suggestions about training active listening were given on p. 92.

Negotiating

Negotiation involves getting people to agree a way forward. This is sometimes a matter of talking to individuals and finding out their views and which ideas are unacceptable to them, which they might be persuaded to accept and which they would welcome. This skill can be trained through the activity described under 'problem-solving interviews' (pp. 98–9). It would involve role-play with a broad plan for a particular piece of work given as the ground for negotiation. Interviewers would then have to interview more than one person to find out the different views held and the areas in which persuasion might work.

Negotiation also goes on within groups: the co-ordinator may find it necessary to explore with the committee the interpretation of different ideas until agreement is reached. Negotiation involves feeling the way forward, being ready to give some ground while holding to other ground, perhaps looking for different routes to the same goal in order to find a route acceptable to those involved.

Planning and organizing

Skill in planning and organizing is needed in order to draw together information about needs and translate it into a programme which can be implemented. It will also be needed for evaluation. The co-ordinator is likely to have the help of the committee in doing this but if he or she is unable to plan and organize the committee will find it difficult to work.

There are a number of planning techniques which the co-ordinator should be aware of. Network analysis was described in Chapter 5 and is a useful way of planning with a group. Force field analysis has also been described and is a useful way of considering the problems involved in making plans.

The use of spreadsheets and databases may also help in the planning process, particularly in a large school where it may be helpful to see clusters of people wanting similar provision.

Chairing a group

Suggestions about training chairpersons were given under 'discussion leadership' (pp. 95–6). The role of the chairperson in a committee responsible for action is rather different from the role of the chairperson in a discussion group, but it is similar in principle. It still involves reacting positively to contributions, drawing together what people say and summing up periodically. It could be practised as a fishbowl activity.

Evaluating

The co-ordinator also has to lead thinking about evaluation. This means having knowledge about the ways in which evaluation can be carried out, both for assessing needs and also for assessing the effectiveness of development activities. These will be covered in Chapter 13. The skills involved are basically those of observation, interviewing and analysis.

Personal support

The teacher undertaking the role of professional development co-ordinator needs support from the headteacher if he or she is to be successful. This means that responsibility should be clearly delegated so that everyone on the staff is aware of what the co-ordinator has been asked to do. It also means making time available and making it possible for the co-ordinator to work with the management of the school where this is appropriate.

Training the trainers

Much of what has been suggested earlier in this book implies that a good deal of professional development work will be an in-school activity with teachers teaching each other. If this is to be effective, some thought needs to be given to helping everyone with the skills of in-service training so that contributions are fully effective. It is much more difficult to make a presentation to a group of one's peers than to a class of children. Adults react in a much more subtle way than children and one has to learn to read the signs that an audience is no longer with one.

Skills of in-service training

The following skills are needed:

1 making a presentation
2 responding to questions
3 leading a discussion group
4 preparing and using handouts
5 presenting pupils' work
6 organizing different kinds of in-service sessions
7 providing opportunities for experiential learning
8 organizing the environment for in-service work.

Suggestions for training a number of the skills required by teachers involved in providing professional development opportunities were given in Chapter 6. Further detail about training these and other skills is given below.

Making a presentation

This was discussed in Chapter 6. Training is mainly a matter of a speaker knowing what makes a good presentation and preparing with these points in mind, observation by another person and feedback to the person giving the presentation.

Responding to questions

There is a skill in managing the question time which normally follows a presentation. It may make more demands on the speaker than the presentation itself. It helps to anticipate the kinds of questions which may be asked and either be prepared for them or include the answers in the talk. Questions may be put directly to the speaker or through a chairperson. Whether the questioning is controlled by speaker or chairperson it is essential to scan the audience so that people sitting at the sides or the back are not left out. It is particularly easy to miss people at the sides near the front.

The way a speaker treats questioners is important. Each questioner should be made to feel that the question he or she is asking is an important one, deserving of a careful answer. Answers should be honest but not dogmatic, giving a range of points of view when this is appropriate. They should not be an occasion for another lecture, which prevents others from asking questions.

These skills, like those of giving the presentation, can be trained by using an observer who gives feedback.

Leading a discussion group

This was dealt with in Chapter 6. The skills of leading discussion are valuable to everyone, especially as some knowledge of the leadership skills tends to make people better discussion group members.

Preparing and using handouts

Handouts are needed for all kinds of activities and their preparation has much in common with preparing worksheets. The advent of desk-top publishing makes it possible to produce much more professional material than was possible in the past.

It is worth remembering that busy teachers are unlikely to read large quantities of text and look to a handout to reduce the task of reading for them. Handouts should be legible, well laid out on the page, with good spaces between passages of text. It is helpful if important items are flagged in some way, so that they are easily spotted.

Before embarking on making a handout, it is helpful to consider how it will be used. (This was discussed in Chapter 6.)

Presenting pupils' work

A very valuable part of the in-service work which teachers can offer each other is the account of work with pupils. This is probably the most common form of general contribution and it has a reality that teachers value. However, it is not altogether easy because much of the work which a teacher might want to show other teachers is too small to use as part of a talk.

There are various ways of tackling this problem. Work can, of course, be read out, but this often loses the quality of the appearance of the work, particularly at the primary stage. When work is read out, it is important for a speaker to be well prepared, with the examples set out in order, so that there are no gaps while he or she turns over papers in search of what is needed. An alternative is to get children to record some of their work and to play the tape. If this is done, it is essential to check that it can be heard from all parts of the room, since children's voices, particularly those of young children, are often too soft when reading in the classroom.

Another alternative is to make transparencies for the overhead projector from some of the work or to take photographs which can be projected. Both of these have the advantage that they provide material which can be used on a number of occasions.

Work can also be set out as an exhibition and the talk can include references to what is on show and time for people to look. The amount exhibited should be limited to what can be shown well. An overcrowded exhibition tends to defeat its purpose. The work looks less good and people are put off by the quantity.

Organizing different kinds of in-service sessions

This was dealt with in some detail in Chapter 6. It helps in training someone to do this if there is an experienced person working alongside, so that each stage and idea can be discussed. The use of a more experienced person as observer is also helpful.

Providing opportunities for experiential learning

It is often tempting when someone is new to providing in-service opportunities to think that the best way of getting information across is to give a talk. In practice teachers are no different from children in this respect. They learn best when they start from their own experience and gain new experience in the area in which they are learning. In-service sessions therefore need to contain substantial opportunities for this kind of activity.

Many of the suggestions given in Chapter 6 provide opportunities for learning through experience and some very simple plans, such as exchanging information about what each person in a group does about something, are often extremely useful. It is helpful to start by thinking of what each person may have to contribute and to build on from there.

Organizing the environment for in-service work

Just as the way the classroom is arranged is important for the learning which is to take place, so the way the space is arranged for in-service work is important. Changes in the organization of space may also be needed in the course of one session. (This was discussed in Chapter 6.)

8

Teacher appraisal

Background

The idea that every teacher should have his or her work appraised every so often has gradually gained adherents in the last few years. Expressions of interest in this approach have come from a number of different quarters and schools are now in the process of introducing it. One of the first indications from government that this would eventually be a requirement was in the White Paper *Teaching Quality*,[62] which stated:

> The Government welcome recent moves towards self-assessment by schools and teachers, and believe these should help to improve school standards and curricula. But employers can manage their teachers only if they have accurate knowledge of each teacher's performance. The Government believe that for this purpose formal assessment of teacher performance is necessary and should be based on classroom visiting by the teacher's head or head of department, and an appraisal of both the pupils' work and of the teacher's contribution to the life of the school. They therefore welcome the interest currently shown among employers and the teachers' associations about the career development of teachers. . . . The Government believe that those responsible for managing the school teacher force have a clear responsibility to establish, in consultation with their teachers, a policy for staff development and training based on a systematic assessment of every teacher's performance and related to their policy for the school curriculum.

Pilot studies were eventually set up in six LEAs and a Circular was issued in 1988 requiring schools to introduce teacher appraisal within the next four years.

Appraisal was finally made compulsory in a letter to Chief Education Officers from the Secretary of State for Education in a letter dated 10 December 1990,[63] in which regulations were laid down for appraisal of all teachers and head-teachers every two years.

All headteachers appraise each teacher's work informally in order to deploy staff and in order to provide information when a teacher is serving the probationary period or is a candidate for promotion. Headteachers and senior staff are continually making judgements about the work of teachers in order to organize the school and decide which teacher will teach which groups of children. They also discuss work with teachers informally and may be consulted about career prospects.

Teachers may seek out and use opportunities to observe, consult and comment on each other's work. A teacher may also discuss with a group of children how they felt about a piece of work, discussing which parts were most interesting, enquiring whether they have ideas about how they could learn better and so on.

These existing practices are valuable and formal appraisal can build on them and make them more systematic.

The study of appraisal made in Suffolk and reported in *Those Having Torches*[64] included the following conclusions about schools where appraisal was successful:

1 the commitment of the head teacher
2 the enthusiasm of the designated appraisers
3 the grasp that teachers had of the nature and intention of the appraisal process
4 that documentation had evolved and was evolving
5 that action followed target-setting
6 that appraisal documentation was used for references and career advice
7 that the documentation was available to teachers at any time.

Also noticeable were

8 the enhanced professionalism of teachers
9 the opening welcoming ethos of the school
10 the willingness of teachers to discuss their appraisal.

HMI in *Quality in Schools*[65] make a similar observation. They say (of appraisal):

The heads commented on high levels of professionalism, greater analysis of practice, a broader educational context against which to make judgments, a receptivity to new ideas and a willingness to explore them. The teachers spoke of the benefits of having to analyse their strengths and weaknesses and of questioning curriculum and methodologies which they had taken for granted for years. They appreciated the opportunity of discussing their performance and career with the head because it improved relations. It also enabled them to see that they had not just a job but a career, which could be developed to take account of their strengths and in which needs could be identified without fear, with a view to their being remedied by appropriate in-service experience.

It would also seem to emerge from experience and from studies of appraisal that it is most likely to succeed where there is an atmosphere of trust in the school, in which people feel that they are valued and that their views are taken seriously. The pilot studies also seem to suggest that appraisal of teachers is easier to introduce in the context of an overall pattern in which there is regular reviewing of the school. The *Report of the Consortium of School Teacher Appraisal Pilot Schemes*[66] quotes Salford, for example, as saying:

> Appraisal is seen as extending links between institutional development and that of individuals. The constructive self-criticism generated by whole school evaluation has created a suitable climate for the identification of schools where appraisal work can develop.

It must also be remembered that many teachers see the idea of appraisal as something of a threat. Ted Wragg[67] notes that 'the fear of a humiliation ritual is one that bedevils the act of appraisal wherever it takes place' and 'the act of appraisal can force people to confront themselves in ways they would normally wish to avoid'. These problems should be kept well in mind in setting up a system of appraisal. There needs to be plenty of opportunity for people to voice their fears and explore ways of meeting them.

Adams and Torrington[68] suggest that

> What most staff want to know is 'how am I doing?' They are frustrated if they feel that no one is interested in their work and they have no sense of being valued. Appraisal schemes will work, and receive staff support, when their main focus is on answering this need for feedback.

All schools are now required by law to state their aims and to publish these in a prospectus. Appraisal of individual teachers is easier where the aims of the school have been discussed, considered and accepted by the whole staff and related to the aims of departments in a secondary school or the parts of the curriculum and different year groups in the primary school. Bollington and Hopkins[69] note that

> The success of appraisal scheme will depend upon those involved coming to a shared understanding of what they are trying to achieve.

They suggest that any LEA or district or school preparing for appraisal 'should make certain that their planning and subsequent action is seen to

1 reflect a high degree of commitment from the policy-making group
2 involve all interested parties in planning for appraisal
3 reflect the educational values of the LEA, local area and school

4 be developmental and explicitly linked to staff development
5 include a methodology for appraisal which is valid, soundly based, utilizes a variety of appraisers and data collection methods, but is *not* prescriptive
6 place a high priority on training, especially for appraisers
7 emphasize the active involvement of teachers, particularly in establishing the rhythm of the process and the setting of criteria.'

Day, Whitaker and Wren[26] suggest five principles which support appraisal.

1 Learning requires opportunities for reflection and self-confrontation.
2 Teachers and schools are motivated to learn by the identification of an issue or a problem which concerns them.
3 Teachers learn best through active experience participation.
4 Decisions about change should arise from reflection upon and confrontation of past and present practice.
5 Schools and teachers need support throughout the processes of change.

The purposes of appraisal

The purposes of appraisal need to be clear to everyone involved. The Secretary of State's letter[63] states that appraisal schemes shall be designed to:

1 help teachers to identify ways of enhancing their professional skill
2 assist in planning the in-service training and professional development of teachers individually and collectively
3 help individual teachers, their headteachers, governing body and local education authorities, (where appropriate) to see where a new or modified assignment would help the professional development of individual teachers and improve their career prospects
4 identify the potential of teachers for career development with the aim of helping them, where possible, through appropriate in-service training
5 provide help to teachers having difficulties with their performance, through appropriate guidance, counselling and training. Disciplinary and dismissal procedures shall remain quite separate but may need to draw on relevant information from appraisal records
6 inform those responsible for providing references for teachers
7 enhance the overall management of schools.

Some other purposes might also be considered:

To provide a means of coordinating the work of the department and the school

Appraisal carried out by those in management roles offers the opportunity to guide the direction of each teacher's work, partly by those things selected out for commendation but also by working with the teacher to agree goals which contribute to the overall goals of the department or school. Appraisal is a source of information to the appraiser about the ways in which people are working.

To provide help and support for teachers in a management role

Teachers in middle management roles in schools often come into these posts at a young age with little or no training in the tasks of management. Part of the training which the school can provide is the opportunity to discuss the tasks of management and to assess progress within them.

To support teachers with management roles in their responsibility for the work of their colleagues

Teachers in management roles are responsible for developing the work of their colleagues. Appraisal makes this responsibility very clear. Teachers in middle management roles will also have to answer for their success in managing this responsibility in their own appraisal.

It provides an opportunity for praising what is good and dealing with unsatisfactory aspects

Anyone in a leadership role needs to offer a considerable amount of praise and encouragement to the colleagues for whom he or she has responsibility. An appraisal system provides a formal opportunity for praising good work.

It can also provide a good context for dealing with the less satisfactory aspects of a teacher's work. When such problems are dealt with in isolation it is very easy for the person on the receiving end to get the matter out of perspective. If it is discussed as part of a full review of work, where some things are good and others less so, most teachers can take the negative points in their stride, especially if a programme is discussed for helping them to overcome the problem.

It provides the teacher with an opportunity to ensure that others know his or her work and for expressing views

Most teachers have a good many comments to make about aspects of the life and work of the school. An appraisal interview offers them the opportunity to express some of these views as well as providing an opportunity to ensure that others are aware of their successes.

It provides the appraiser with additional knowledge about what is happening and enables him or her to have a view of the department or school as a whole

The appraisal interview is an excellent way of getting information not only about factual aspects of what is happening, but also about the way individual teachers are seeing things and the ideas and views they hold about the school and their own part in it.

Knowledge of the views and plans of different teachers often enable a head or head of department to link the work different people are doing.

It is an opportunity for the person in a leadership role to influence the thinking of each teacher and to be influenced by teachers' views

Leadership involves weaving together the thinking of colleagues to make a coherent whole. This may mean persuading some people to move towards each other or explaining why something is not possible. It also gives the appraiser a chance to share his or her view of the whole, with each teacher. This gives teachers an insight into where their work fits into the total pattern. Equally the leader may be influenced by an individual teacher.

The pre-conditions for introducing appraisal

Change is not easy and the introduction of appraisal needs careful and thoughtful planning if it is to be successful.

Egan[70] notes some of the problems involved in change, which are particularly relevant to the move to appraisal:

1 It is not easy to receive help.
2 It is difficult to commit oneself to change.
3 It is difficult to submit to the influence of a helper; help is a threat to esteem, integrity and independence.
4 It is not easy to trust a stranger and be open with him or her.
5 It is not easy to see one's problems clearly at first.
6 Sometimes problems seem too large, too overwhelming or too unique to share easily.

Prevailing conditions

If a staff appraisal scheme is to work well, there needs to be certain conditions present at the beginning. The following points should be considered.

There should be a measure of consensus about values among those involved

Values should be discussed and consensus achieved as far as possible. Where there cannot be consensus there should be respect for differences and an ability to make judgements taking the differences into account.

There needs to be an atmosphere of trust

Individual appraisal is doomed to failure if those involved do not respect each other's professionalism. Teachers being appraised need to be confident that the information they give will not be used for purposes other than those agreed without further consultation.

Those involved need to be open-minded

Much can be learnt from all parties in appraisal if everyone is open to anything which can be learned in the process. The opportunity for learning is there not only for the person being appraised but also for the person doing the appraising.

The teacher's self-image is important

A teacher with a poor view of his or her own work will find it difficult to use the experience of appraisal in positive ways. It may be necessary in introducing such a system to work first to help teachers to think well of themselves.

The organizational climate needs to be positive

It should be concerned with helping teachers to give of their best and developing their full potential.

A clear job description is needed for each teacher

This provides agreed objectives against which performance can be assessed.

The expected outcomes of appraisal should be clearly defined at the outset

In particular teachers need to be aware of the use likely to be made of the information gained.

Both parties need to prepare for the appraisal meeting

It is therefore necessary for there to be agreement about the ground to be covered.

Principles for professional development

One school, setting out its professional development policy, identified three main principles and a number of subsidiary ones which they regarded as necessary for the policy to have meaning. See Montgomery.[71]

The three main principles are as follows:

1 We strive to create an environment of trust.
2 We believe that all teachers are capable of development and change.
3 We remain positive and optimistic.

Further principles (abridged) were as follows:

1 Delegate responsibility wherever possible encourage staff to accept corporate responsibility for what goes on in the school.
2 Foster the feeling of trust and loyalty. We recognize that this is the foundation on which we build, in order that constructive criticism and divergence of views may flourish.
3 Encourage staff to become involved in educational issues, curriculum change and its implementation.
4 Provide support and counselling for individual teachers.
5 Encourage open dialogue between all staff.
6 Make in-service provision available as appropriate to individual staff, small groups and the entire staff.
7 Provide praise, encouragement and critical feedback to help staff develop a critical approach to their work.
8 Provide opportunities for increased job satisfaction, develop a wider range of skills and thereby increase opportunities for promotion at a time of contraction.

It is likely that appraisal will be most successful in improving performance where the teacher has some control over what happens. All aspects of appraisal need whole staff discussion with everyone involved in the decisions made. There is also a need for discussion with individuals about what is to be appraised, although it must be remembered that teachers may not be willing to tackle their own weak points and it may be difficult for the head or other senior member of the staff to help someone who insists that all is well. This may be overcome by allowing for both parties to be involved in deciding the aspects they wish to tackle.

Planning appraisal

There are a large number of questions which need to be tackled in planning an appraisal scheme and many of them are best discussed by the staff as a whole. The Secretary of State's letter[63] says:

The appraiser of a teacher shall be a person designated by the head-teacher or the headteacher him or herself.

This would seem to imply that appraisal should be carried out by someone senior to the teacher in question, although there is nothing in the statement which prevents peer group appraisal or appraisal by someone of the teacher's own choice, provided these are agreed by the headteacher. It should be remembered, however, that it is unlikely that such schemes will be acceptable to those outside the school, including the school governors because they are likely to be seen as a soft option.

At each stage of appraisal various kinds of forms will be needed. There are many examples available and some are given in the Appendices. A very useful collection is given in the Suffolk Education Department document *Teacher Appraisal: A Practical Guide, Part 3*.[72]

The following questions need to be considered:

1 What overall organization do we need?
2 What ground should appraisal cover?
3 Who should appraise whom?
4 When and how often should it take place?
5 What classroom observation should take place? Who should undertake it? When should it take place?
6 What methods of observation should be used?
7 What other evidence should be used?
8 What preparation for appraisal should be carried out by the teacher and the appraiser?
9 What use should be made of the job description?
10 What use should be made of target setting?
11 What interviews are needed?
12 How can fairness be maintained between teachers? What happens about the bad appraiser?
13 What records should be kept? To whom should they be available? What use should be made of them? How long should they be kept? Who has ownership of them? How confidential are they?
14 Will the record be used for disciplinary purposes?
15 What follow-up should there be?
16 What is the cost of appraisal in terms of time? How can this be found?

What overall organization do we need?

When appraisal is introduced into a school there is a good deal to be done and there needs to be some organization which involves as many people as possible in the process. One way of doing this is to create a committee of which each member is a chairperson of a working group looking at a particular aspect of appraisal. In a secondary school this could involve everyone in one of the working groups, except where the school is very large. In a very large school it might make sense to have more than one working group looking at each aspect and to bring their findings together at the later stage. In a primary school, people might need to work in pairs rather than groups and it may be that everyone is a member of the appraisal committee, depending on the size of the school. The following topics might be appropriate for the working groups.

1 Classroom observation – types of observation, recording.
2 Feedback on classroom observation – what is useful to discuss and how it is best undertaken?
3 Collecting information about a teacher's performance in pastoral care as a form tutor or class teacher.
4 Other information about a teacher's work – extra-curricular activities, contribution to the life of the school, etc.
5 Preparation for appraisal interviews – task of self-evaluation, forms for completion.
6 Recording the appraisal interview – record forms, their use, etc.

What ground should appraisal cover?

Teachers need to know what particular aspects of their work are being appraised and the way the evidence is to be collected. The following might be covered:

1 teaching performance
2 pastoral work
3 management responsibilities and skills (where appropriate)
4 professional development
5 potential and career development
6 other contributions to the school (e.g. extra-curricular activities).

In the context of discussing these issues an appraiser may well wish to discuss interpersonal relationships with a teacher, particularly if these are impeding the teacher's progress with children or with colleagues.

Decisions about the way information is to be collected will need to be made. Classroom observation would seem to be essential but are there to be several visits or only one? Are they to be unexpected or will the teacher know when they are taking place? Who decides which lessons are visited? Similarly a secondary school will need to decide what to do about appraising work as a form tutor and a primary school will need to consider a teacher's competence in managing the non-teaching aspects of being a class teacher. There must also be a decision about how work in extra-curricular activities is to be assessed.

Who should appraise whom?

The Secretary of State[63] has determined that this should be the headteacher or someone designated by him or her. This would seem to imply a form of appraisal in which teachers are appraised by those senior to them but leaves open other possibilities if the headteacher agrees with them.

It is generally accepted that one appraiser should not have to deal with more than six or seven people, since it is unreasonable to expect one person to undertake the preparation and observation involved for more than this. This means that in a secondary school and in a large primary school there will be a number of people involved, all of whom will need training in the skills of conducting appraisal.

David Trethowan[18] makes a very strong case for the person appraising another to be in a line management relationship with that person. He sets down the following rules:

1 Every member of staff has a manager to whom he or she is accountable and who is responsible for the teacher's performance.
2 There is no dual accountability. Teachers may work for more than one department but are managed and appraised by one person only.
3 No appraiser manages more than seven people effectively.
4 Every member of staff is aware of the basic task he or she is required to perform.
5 There is a hierarchical organizational structure for the school in which levels of responsibility are clearly defined and a clear understanding exists of how each post relates to the whole.

In a small primary school the question of who should appraise whom is not a difficult one. The headteacher is the person in a line manager role to all the staff and he or she may appraise everyone, or share this activity with the deputy so that the deputy gets the experience of undertaking appraisal. In a large primary school, this will not be so easy and the headteacher may wish to share the tasks of appraisal, not only with the deputy, but also with one or two other senior members of staff. This poses a problem because most teachers will want to be appraised by the headteacher. One way of overcoming this problem is for the headteacher to appraise everyone on alternative occasions, with someone else undertaking the appraisal in between.

In a secondary school the most obvious pattern is one in which the heads of department appraise their department staff and the headteacher and deputies appraise the heads of department, unless there is a faculty organization, in which case the heads of faculty appraise the heads of department and the headteacher and deputies appraise the faculty heads. The advantage of this is that people in line management roles have the opportunity to guide and support their own staff. A disadvantage is that not all heads of department will be credible as appraisers, although good training will help. There is also the problem of the teacher who works in more than one department. Probably the best way to deal with this is to decide that the head of one of the departments is responsible for that teacher and for his or her appraisal.

Other schemes which have been tried involve teachers choosing their appraiser from a small number of appropriate people. The advantage of this is that teachers may feel much happier about the whole process. The disadvantage is that the person in the line manager role does not have the opportunities which appraisal offers to find out about what is happening and to influence it. A further disadvantage is that teachers may well select someone not familiar with the subjects or age groups they teach and therefore at a disadvantage when it comes to providing support. There could also be a good deal of bitterness on the part of those appraisers not chosen and this could make for difficult relationships in the future.

Two further problems which the secondary school will experience are the single teacher department and that of appraising work as a form tutor. Heads of department may also have more senior people, such as deputies, teaching in their department.

To some extent the single teacher department is being overcome by the formation of faculties in many schools. This organization also gives an extra layer of people who might be part of the appraisal plan. Alternatively the single member of a department should be appraised by a senior member of staff.

There are various ways of tackling the form tutor problem. Appraisal on alternate occasions might be undertaken by the year head or whoever is responsible for form tutors and might concentrate on this aspect of the teacher's work. Or the year head might feed information to the person doing the appraisal.

Where a deputy or other senior member of the staff works within a department, it would seem to make sense that the head of department sees that teacher at work in the classroom as should be the case with any other member of the department, and offers feedback but is not responsible for appraisal.

An appraisal system needs a built-in check. It may be a good idea to adopt the grandfather (or grandmother) system whereby the appraiser's appraiser receives and signs copies of the reports of the appraisals undertaken by the people he or she appraises and takes some responsibility for their performances as appraisers.

When and how often should it take place?

The Secretary of State has decided that appraisal should take place for each teacher every two years. He also suggests that

> in the second year of the cycle the appraiser and appraisee shall meet to review the appraisal statement and progress in achieving agreed targets.

No suggestions have yet been given about teachers in their probationary year who are not included in the overall plans for appraisal. For these teachers, a review each term might be helpful, looking at how things have gone and agreeing some targets for the coming term. This would not be appraisal in the normal sense, but part of the induction programme.

Teachers new to the school might also be given the opportunity to discuss their work more frequently in their first year.

Appraisal for each teacher every other year makes the pressure of time rather less a matter for concern. The time taken for follow-up will be much less than that for a full appraisal.

For secondary schools the best time for appraisal would seem to be the second half of the summer term when the year's work can be discussed, and it may be possible to fit this in with the many tasks the school undertakes after examinations. In a primary school this may be more difficult, because the second half of the summer term tends to be a time for field study and open days and other events. In practice, appraisal may have to go on all the year round.

What classroom observation should take place? Who should undertake it? When should it take place?

The Secretary of State has decreed that classroom observation should take place on at least two occasions. In planning appraisal, decisions need to be made about such matters of who observes each teacher, length of observations to be made and whether the teacher has any say in which lessons will be observed and whether he or she will be informed in advance. There also needs to be a decision about feedback – when it should take place.

What methods of observation should be used?

Details of methods of observation are given in Chapter 9. Decisions should be made about which to use.

What other evidence should be used?

Other possible evidence will include the pupils' work, including examination results where appropriate and in future test results at different stages. Evidence of the pupils' views might also be sought and used. Pastoral work will provide evidence. So will competence in the administrative tasks required of classroom teachers and extra-curricular work. Teachers in management roles should expect to be appraised on the skill with which they undertake their management tasks and particularly on their ability to manage other people well.

What preparation for appraisal should be carried out by the teacher and the appraiser?

This is discussed in Chapter 10. It may be noted here that preparation is necessary for both parties and that there are some suggested forms in Appendix 1.

What use should be made of the job description?

The job description can be a useful starting-point and form of check-list for appraisal against which both teacher and appraiser can make judgements. If it is to be used in this way, however, it must set out clearly the tasks or account-abilities involved in an individual teacher's job.

What use should be made of target-setting?

There is much to be said for each teacher agreeing a number of goals or targets with the appraiser. This helps to define what needs to be done and gives one measure against which work can be judged. Details of target-setting are given in Chapter 10.

What interviews are needed?

A main interview is needed for appraisal but some schools have found it helpful to have a preliminary interview to discuss what will be needed for the main interview. This can be avoided to some extent if there is clear general agreement on what is to be appraised.

The regulations require a follow-up interview to find out how things are going. This will be helpful for everyone but may be particularly valuable for those who need encouragement to keep on course. The follow-up interview would look at the way the professional development programme was going and the way the individual teacher was managing to work towards goals.

How can fairness be maintained between teachers? What happens about the bad appraiser?

The question of fairness between teachers is a difficult one because it is impossible to treat everyone in exactly the same way. Each appraiser will have a different style and way of tackling the task and interviews will also differ according to the relationship of the people involved. However, it should be possible through training to make appraisers aware of the specific tasks involved and a range of good ways to tackle them. It is also possible to agree that specific ground will be covered and that comparable information will be used for each teacher. The 'grandparent' system will also help to create similarity of performance.

In any school it is possible that there will be appraisers who are not very good at what they are doing in spite of training. This poses problems for the teachers they appraise and devalues the system, since the teachers appraised by indifferent appraisers will not value the activity or even take it seriously. Although this problem can be overcome to some extent by allowing teachers to choose their appraisers from a number of staff, this practice does nothing to improve the performance of bad appraisers and, as we have already noted, the concept of line managers supporting the teachers for whom they are responsible is partially lost.

There are two people who can do something about the bad appraiser. These are the teacher being appraised and the person responsible for the appraisal of the appraiser concerned. The teacher should give the indifferent appraiser feedback about the ways in which he or she seems to be bad and look for ways in which the appraiser can be encouraged or supported. If necessary the teacher should talk to the appraiser's appraiser about the problems. The appraiser's appraiser should be aware of the difficulties and should take an opportunity as part of appraisal or otherwise, to discuss the whole problem and try to suggest ways in which improvement might be achieved. Role-play might be helpful here with feedback on what it seems like from the point of view of the person being appraised.

What records should be kept? To whom should they be available? What use should be made of them? How long should they be kept? Who owns them? How confidential will they be? Will they be used for writing references? Will they be used in disciplinary cases?

The Secretary of State has designated the people to whom records will be available as follows:

> The appraiser shall give a copy of the appraisal statement to the head-teacher of the school. In the case of teachers at LEA maintained schools, the headteacher shall give a copy to the Chief Education Officer of the Authority and any LEA officer or adviser specifically designated by him or her. In addition the headteacher shall make a copy of the statement available to any person responsible for considering a complaint by the appraisee.
>
> The appraiser shall record targets for action decided at the appraisal interview in a separate annex from the rest of the appraisal statement. The headteacher shall give a copy of the targets, but not the rest of the statement, to the chairman of governors of the school if he or she so requests.

The regulations also make it clear that appraisal reports will be used for writing references and where appropriate this material may be drawn on in cases of disciplinary procedures.

Appraisal records should be kept for a limited time only, partly because they will quickly become out of date and partly because of the space they will take up. Some decision needs to be made about this. There is also the question of what happens at the end of that period and also the occasion when a teacher leaves for another school or for retirement or for some other reason. If the teacher owns the record, then it should be handed back to him or her when it runs out of time or when the teacher leaves. On the other hand the school may wish to retain a copy of the last report on a teacher leaving in case there is a request for a confidential report on that teacher. This should be negotiated. Suggested forms for appraisal records are given in Appendix 3.

What follow-up should there be?

We have already noted that there is to be a follow-up meeting to discuss progress. The statement about the purposes of appraisal makes it clear that appraisal should be followed by a programme of professional development designed to match the needs of the individual. This may be a programme of in-service training but does not necessarily have to be so. Many of the kinds of activities outlined in Chapter 2 would provide such a programme and there are many opportunities for people to develop as part of the ordinary life of the school. There should, if possible, be some kind of check-up in the course of the year that the programme designed is running satisfactorily and that work towards any goal is proceeding.

What is the cost of appraisal in terms of time? How can this be found?

The letter of the Secretary of State believes that the only time extra which is needed is that for classroom observation. His view is that time for appraisal and for training can be found within directed time. Other surveys suggest that the cost of appraisal in terms of time is considerable. The Suffolk paper *In the Light of Torches*[73] gives a detailed breakdown of the time likely to be needed; it is shown in Table 1.

It will undoubtedly be necessary to consider ways of organizing the work of the school to make appraisal possible. In a secondary school this may be a matter of having larger groups for some work in order to give people more free time to undertake appraisal. It will be more difficult to find time in a primary

Table 1   Time required for an appraisal

	Appraiser	Appraisee
Classroom observation	120 mins (3 lessons)	
Writing up (and discussion)	30 mins	30 mins
Preliminary interview	30 mins	30 mins
Main interview	60 mins	60 mins
Follow-up if necessary	30 mins	30 mins
Totals	270 mins (3½ hours)	150 mins (2½ hours)

school, although here too it is possible to have larger classes and use teachers who are not class teachers to support those who are and to provide the opportunity for developmental work and appraisal. The only other alternative if extra staffing is not provided for appraisal is to hold the discussions after school, but as part of directed time. This still leaves the problem of observing classroom work. This will be easiest in a small school where the headteacher is free of a class and is doing all the appraisal, although it clearly takes time from other tasks the headteacher might be doing. It is more difficult where other teachers need to be involved or in a very small school where the headteacher has a full-time role as classroom teacher.

A school will also need to explain the appraisal programme to governors and to parents. Governors should be kept informed about the progress of the scheme as it is introduced. The headteacher and teachers may wish to feel some confidence in what is happening before parents are told about it officially, but the presence of parent governors will mean that information is widely available: it may therefore be better to keep parents informed from an early stage.

The appraisal of headteachers

One of the most difficult aspects of appraisal is the appraisal of headteachers. It is difficult because the head's job is large and complex and because the management lines are not clearly defined. Headteachers are responsible both to their governors and to the chief education officer of their LEA; many heads would also claim that they are responsible to their pupils and their parents. This makes it difficult to decide on the right person to conduct headteacher appraisal.

The regulations[63] state:

> Headteachers of county, controlled and special agreement schools shall be appraised by two persons appointed by the local education authority, after consultation with the governing body of the school.
> Headteachers of voluntary aided schools shall be appraised by two persons appointed jointly by the governing body of the school and the local education authority. If the LEA and the governing body cannot agree on the selection of appraisers, the appraisal is to be carried out by one person appointed by the governing body and one appointed by the LEA.
> Headteachers of grant-maintained schools and non-maintained schools shall be appraised by two persons appointed by the governing body of the school.
> The appraisers of a headteacher shall include one person with experience as a headteacher relevant to current conditions in the type of school – primary, secondary or special – in which the appraisee headteacher works.

Bollington and Hopkins in their review of research[69] suggest the following criteria for selecting people for headship appraisal:

1 *Credibility* Appraisers will need to be credible to headteachers yet also credible to other interested parties including 'the observer on the top deck of the Clapham omnibus'.[73]
2 *Consistency* The decision on who appraises headteachers cannot be seen in isolation from who appraises teachers. The implications of adopting a line management model for teacher appraisal would make it very difficult to adopt a peer appraisal for headteachers.
3 *Competence* The question here is: do appraisers have sufficient knowledge and awareness of the headteacher's job to be in a position to offer adequate diagnosis and support?
4 *Capability* Given the commitment in the ACAS principles to following-up appraisal and evidence from industry that schemes failing in this respect lose credibility, are appraisers in a position to guarantee delivery of identified needs of in-service development?

The size of even small LEAs makes it impossible to consider a line management model in the normal sense for headteacher appraisal. Chief education officers, even in small authorities, would be unable to appraise all the headteachers for whom they are responsible; most are not sufficiently close to the day-to-day work of the headteacher to meet the competence requirement above.

The *ACAS Report of the Appraisal and Training Working Group*[74] suggested that anyone appraising headteachers should have had headship experience. This might be interpreted as another way of saying that the appraiser must be credible. There are people with headship experience who would not be credible and others without it who would be acceptable. Peer group appraisal would not meet the consistency requirement and might not be able to meet that of capability as defined above. Not all headteachers are anxious to be appraised by their peers although the interim *Report of the Consortium of School Teacher Appraisal Pilot Schemes*[66] found this to be the preferred option. Where headteachers are unenthusiastic about peer group appraisal it is sometimes because they are uncertain about the colleague they will get. This concern can be met by offering each headteacher a choice of appraisers from a panel, perhaps chosen by the LEA. The other reason why some headteachers would prefer to be appraised by an adviser or an education officer (if they have credibility) is that they can see that it could be helpful to be appraised by someone who has the capability defined above and could take action about some of the points which may come out in appraisal. The LEA may also feel that there is a case for being involved in headteacher appraisal as part of the task of evaluating schools.

The first Suffolk study, *Those Having Torches*,[64] suggested that a level of 'promoted' head should be appointed for this purpose. The second study, *In the Light of Torches*,[73] explored the possibility of subordinate appraisal. This has much to commend it but not only is it inconsistent with the way teachers are appraised but also it is unlikely to be as acceptable as appraisal by someone not working in the school, since it carries with it the danger that some subordinates will not speak freely.

The Secretary of State's decisions about the people to act as headteacher appraisers has been supported by the Suffolk study *In the Light of Torches* and many of the studies in the pilot scheme also suggest a small team which includes a practising headteacher of the same phase and a representative of the chief education officer, probably the school's general adviser. This would seem to be a fair compromise. This team is expected to interview the staff, governors and parents and to consult with appropriate education officers and advisers. The Somerset pilot scheme (*Review and Development − Progress Report*)[75] suggests that primary headteachers should be observed teaching and secondary headteachers observed taking assembly and chairing a meeting. The regulations require that the headteacher is either seen teaching or 'doing some other work'.

Appraisal by a team has the disadvantage of being expensive in time, especially as calculated by the Suffolk paper.

Useful documents for headship appraisal are found in *In the Light of Torches*[73] and in *Appraisal and Target Setting* by David Trethowan.[18]

Training for appraisal

If appraisal is to be successful, those conducting it need to acquire the necessary skills and those experiencing it need to know the details of what is involved.

When a school first undertakes appraisal the training need is evident and in a secondary school there will be sufficient people involved in appraising to make it possible to run courses especially for them. Primary schools will need to link together to provide such training which will normally be the responsibility of the LEA. Once appraisal is under way in a school, however, it will be much more difficult to provide the necessary training for those coming new to the task of appraising others and those coming new into the school or the profession.

David Trethowan[18] suggests that a good starting-point for appraisal training is to build an audit of skills which will be required by teachers generally and by those conducting appraisal. Such an audit was given in Chapter 4 as part of provision for needs assessment.

A good deal of emphasis has been placed on the need to involve teachers in developing the appraisal pattern in the school; this in itself constitutes a form of training, since it enables everyone to know what will be taking place. There are also a number of ways in which those who will experience appraisal and those who will appraise can look together at aspects of appraisal. For example a useful in-service activity to be undertaken in small groups is to list the characteristics of a good appraisal interview. These can then be gathered together and a number of them discussed in detail and their implications for appraisers noted.

It may also be useful to look together at classroom observation, looking at different types of observation, building possible check-lists and clarifying ideas about what can be observed.

Preparation for appraisal is another area which can be discussed and forms can be mutually designed and agreed.

Teachers who have been involved in this kind of activity will gradually cease to see appraisal as threatening because it will become known and familiar. This would seem to be one of the best ways of preparing teachers for appraisal.

Other parts of the process will need more direct training. For example teachers may need help and practice in setting objectives. Most people tend to set objectives which are really aims at first and need help in clarifying what they are saying so that the objective can be seen to be achieved.

Those who will be involved in appraising others will need further training. They may need further work on classroom observation, particularly in terms of the kind of feedback they might give to the teacher concerned. They will also need training in aspects of appraisal interviewing. Both of these activities are most easily trained through role-play and follow-up discussion. Each of the aspects of the appraisal interview listed in Chapter 10 can be role-played, for example the stages of the interview, being direct and goal-setting. This will involve developing characters who pose particular kinds of problems for the interviewer. Interviews should involve three people, an interviewer, an interviewee and an observer who makes notes during the interview and gives feedback afterwards. This should be a selection of important points where possible presented as questions, not a blow-by-blow account of what happened. The observer's feedback should also lead to feedback from the interviewee, who describes how he or she felt about the way the interview went.

Most people find being direct quite difficult and it is often more difficult in role-play than in real life. There is a tendency to avoid saying something which might be hurtful even though it is accepted that it needs to be said. It is often helpful to play over again different pieces of the role-play to see if the interviewer can improve the second time round.

Once appraisal is established in a school there will not be the same need for teachers coming new to the staff to experience training designed to reassure them about it because if it is going well, other teachers will do this. They will need careful briefing on what is involved, however, and this should be someone's responsibility. It could be the responsibility of the teacher's line manager in a secondary school and the headteacher or deputy in a primary school. Alternatively the co-ordinator for professional development or some other senior teacher could undertake this task.

Teachers coming new into senior posts which involve appraising others will need some of the kind of training suggested above. In a secondary school there may be several people coming into such posts at the same time and there may also be a case for offering training to people coming up to this level – to those second in department, for example. It may therefore be possible to make a group of a reasonable size for training on a number of occasions and for the headteacher or other senior staff to run the course. A small secondary school will find this more difficult and may need to link with another school to make provision and so will primary schools where it may be the headteacher coming into post with no knowledge or experience of appraising others. This really requires provision on the part of the LEA and headteachers requiring training should ask about it. It may also be possible to find and attend a national course. Alternatively a group of primary school headteachers might get together and invite a course tutor to run a course for them.

9

Appraisal: observing teachers at work

The person responsible for appraising another teacher's work is likely in many schools to be the person who has line responsibility for that teacher. In this role the appraiser is therefore responsible for supporting and encouraging the teacher concerned and should know a great deal about his or her work already.

Criteria for an appraisal

If judgements about the work of individual teachers are to be acceptable to them, a shared set of criteria is required which has been worked out by the staff of a school. There should be agreed statements about the following criteria.

What constitutes good teaching

While it is appreciated that there are many successful ways of teaching, there should be some agreement about many aspects. The discussion of this topic in itself is a valuable professional development exercise.

What constitutes effective behaviour in a management role

This needs to be discussed and decided upon by those teachers in management roles in the school. It may be helpful to include in the group discussing this some teachers who are among the managed, since they will have a view about what constitutes good management from their angle.

Effective performance as a form tutor or class teacher

Although this mainly concerns secondary schools, primary school class teachers also have a pastoral role which needs to be considered.

What should be included about other aspects of a teacher's work

Teachers do many things in school besides teaching. There should be discussion of these and agreement about how far and in what way they should contribute to the information gathered for appraisal.

School evaluation schemes

Some of the pilot schemes of appraisal make the point that appraisal of individual teachers is most effective in the context of overall reviewing of the school. This introduces evaluation in a more impersonal fashion and provides a background. Many LEAs have school evaluation schemes and a number of these are available to people outside the Authority. Many schools have found that the GRIDS[40] scheme (*Guidelines for Review and Institutional Development*) a very valuable tool, since it involves the whole staff in decisions about evaluation.

Sources of information for the appraisal

There are a number of specific sources on which the appraiser can draw in collecting information for the appraisal interview:

1 self-assessment by the teacher concerned
2 planned observation of the teacher's work in the classroom
3 test and examination results
4 study of children's work
5 information from pupils
6 observation of teacher in a pastoral role
7 observation of teacher in a management role
8 other observation.

Self-assessment by the teacher concerned

Teacher appraisal needs to be closely linked with self-assessment so that a teacher comes to appraisal having thought about work over the previous months and with plans for the future. This is something which a good teacher does all the time. The appraisal process involves making this much more intentional and systematic by offering teachers some tools for observation.

In one school, where the headteacher held a regular review meeting with each member of staff, he sent out a paper to everyone he was due to see which started by saying:

> The purpose of this document is to create a framework for our review of your work in such a way that it creates:
> - an opportunity for you to think through and evaluate your aims, objectives and practices
> - an agenda for us to work together on a programme of development and consolidation over a period of time.

Self-evaluation by an individual teacher can be of two main kinds. It may be the evaluation of a particular lesson or lessons or it may be more general.

There is now a good deal of material about to assist teachers in their own self-evaluation. There are many self-evaluation forms in the literature on which a school can draw in making an appropriate design. The Suffolk papers in particular have many suggestions (*In the Light of Torches*[73] and *Teacher Appraisal: A Practical Guide, Part 3*[72]). Many LEAs have published check-lists of various kinds for the use of schools. Most of the materials published as a result of the pilot scheme for appraisal include the forms used; some suggested forms are given in Appendix 1. There is much to be said for a school agreeing the areas in which teachers might be expected to undertake self-evaluation. There is also much value in groups of teachers building their own check-lists.

Many self-evaluation forms can also be used by an observer who completes the same form on behalf of the teacher observed. Teacher and observer can then discuss the areas in which ratings differ.

Planned observation of the teacher's work in the classroom

The most important part of any teacher's work is within the classroom. Teachers are likely to benefit and increase ability to develop strengths and to analyse any areas of difficulty if they experience careful observation by a sympathetic colleague. This should be a positive and helpful experience designed to reflect what is happening from another point of view.

Effect of the observer

It is very important for anyone acting as observer to be as sympathetic and to be as unobtrusive as possible. At the same time, it has to be acknowledged that the presence of another teacher in the room, particularly a teacher in a senior role in the school, will affect the way the children behave and this has to be allowed for. This is less likely to be a problem if classroom observation of other teachers' lessons is a normal practice in the school and not simply something which happens in the context of appraisal. Probationers and main professional grade teachers can learn from observing other teachers at work and will have their own contribution to make to what is observed.

Feedback

The Somerset Progress Report[75] of their pilot study of appraisal suggests that feedback on classroom observation should focus on

1 performance rather than personality
2 observations rather than assumptions, inferences or explanations
3 descriptions rather than judgements
4 the specific and concrete rather than the general and the abstract
5 the present rather than the past
6 sharing information rather than giving advice
7 alternatives rather than 'what you should do is . . .'
8 the individual's needs
9 requests from the individual.

This is useful general advice, appropriate for the vast majority of teachers, but there will be situations, particularly with teachers who are having difficulty, when the advice may need to be more prescriptive than these points suggest. An experienced teacher has valuable advice to offer to an inexperienced teacher and most teachers have benefited from this kind of help from colleagues in their early days of teaching. Most teachers also welcome it when a senior colleague says work is good. At the same time it is important that discussion following classroom observation should take into account differences in teaching style and recognize that it may be unhelpful for one teacher to tell another how he or she would deal with a situation because their styles may be different.

Ways of observing

There are a number of ways of observing in classrooms and it is important that anyone observing is clear about what he or she is trying to do. Ted Wragg[67] suggests that in looking at classroom competence one is normally looking at

1 the behaviour and experiences of the pupils (worthwhileness of task, on-task behaviour, match)
2 the behaviour of the teacher (professional skills of ability to explain, question, manage children's behaviour, prepare, organize, assess and monitor progress).

He also suggests some key subheadings for observation:

• preparation and planning
• teacher's questions
• explaining
• class management
• observing pupils.

Rating scales

One way of observing is to use a rating scale. Here the observer goes into the classroom with a list of things to observe and rates the extent and the level at which they appear to be present. A pro forma is needed for this and the observer must have a clear idea in mind about what each item listed actually means in practice.

Rating scales can involve what is known as high inference or low inference. They can include items which require little or no interpretation, e.g. 'teacher speaks to pupil' (low inference) or they can involve considerable interpretation, e.g. 'work is well-matched to pupils' (high inference). The extent to which any scale uses one or the other depends to some extent on the purpose of the observation. It is likely that observation for appraisal will include many high-inference items; it must be remembered that a teacher being observed may make different inferences from the observer. These differences are usually a fruitful area for discussion.

The advantage of this kind of observation is that it gives a clear basis for making observations and for the conclusions reached. The disadvantage is that the observer is dictated to by the list and may miss other things which are important.

Although there are many appropriate check-lists on the market and one is included in Appendix 2, groups of teachers often gain a good deal by making their own. Day, Whitaker and Wren[26] give the following list of suggestions for teachers making their own check-lists for observation

1 identify purpose
2 establish focus – yourself, a group of children, the class, individual children
3 determine the criteria of quality and effectiveness
4 assess feasibility – can you observe it?
5 consider validity – how can you check for bias etc?
6 decide on a time frame
7 determine categories.

Narrative method

An alternative approach is to use a narrative in which the observer notes points which seem significant, with or without a particular set of ideas in mind. An observer might, for example, be concerned with the questioning techniques a teacher uses for a time, noting the extent of the use of open and closed questions, recall questions, questions which make pupils think things out for themselves and so on. Or the techniques the teacher uses to control the class and their effectiveness might be observed, noting such matters as the extent to which the teacher praises pupils for doing the right thing as distinct from speaking to those who are not conforming; whether there are pupils who never get noticed; the extent to which the teacher is enhancing the pupil's thinking ability; whether the boys are treated or behave differently from the girls. Such points can be noted for later discussion.

There is some interesting work on observation narratives in *Evaluation and Enhancement of Teaching Performance* by Diane Montgomery.[71] This involves classroom observation by an observer who is trained to observe particular things. The activity works on two levels in that the observer is both looking at how the teacher is enabling the pupils to learn but is also applying the same principles to the teacher's learning.

The scheme also involves what is called 'Tactical lesson planning', which involves lesson planning with particular emphasis on clarity of objectives and on detail planning of changes of activity. There are three critical factors in this activity:

1 developing positive self-images in the pupils and in the teachers
2 stimulating thinking and communication through the medium of any subject or through skills training
3 engaging in tactical lesson planning.

Three principles underlie the consultant's behaviour and subsequent discussion with the teacher: CBG, PCI and 3Ms.

Catch them Being Good (CBG)

The idea here is for the teacher to look out for opportunities to tell pupils individually that they are doing well and are on the right lines, in behaviour as well as work. At the same time the observer is applying this principle to noting the activity of the teacher and is recording the good things that the teacher does.

Positive Cognitive Intervention (PCI)

Learners do better when they are involved in the material they are learning. This is most likely when their own experience and knowledge is used to lead into new learning and where the learning is immediately applied for a purpose or used in problem-solving. The observer notes the occasions when the teacher does something which extends the pupil's thinking.

Management, Monitoring and Maintenance (3 Ms)

This is concerned with the way the teacher gains and maintains attention from the pupils, deals with problems and interruptions, changes of activity and manages their learning. The observer notes what happens within the lesson, writing a narrative according to this pattern and at the end shares the observation with the teacher with emphasis on looking at the operation of the principles set out earlier.

Triangulation

There has been a good deal of work in various places involving teachers working in groups observing and evaluating each other's work. John Elliott[76] describes a technique which he calls 'triangulation' as 'bringing different kinds of evidence into some relationship so that they can be compared and monitored'.

He goes on to describe the basic principles of triangulation as that of collecting observations/accounts of a situation (or some aspects of it) from a variety of angles and perspectives and then comparing and contrasting them. For example, a teacher can compare and contrast accounts of teaching acts in the classroom from his or her own, the pupils' and an observer's point of view.

Elliott lists a range of ways of collecting evidence about what happened, including such ideas as diaries, profiles of what happened over time, document analysis, photographs, video and audio tape, transcripts and interviews. The triangulation process involves comparing the different accounts noting the points where they differ, agree and disagree.

The extended professional teacher

Another scheme which was concerned with evaluating a teacher's work more broadly was developed by a small OECD conference in 1979. This conference set out to try to define the characteristics of the 'thinking school' and the 'extended professional' teacher. These were summed up in each case by a series of brief sentences:

The extended professional teacher should

- be competent in the classroom
- have sound relationships with pupils
- be conscientious in discharge of duties
- be professionally aware
- be skilled in observing pupils and in interpreting observations
- have strategies for problem-solving
- see work in the wider context
- contribute to curriculum development
- be able to support practice with theory
- collaborate with colleagues
- be able to contribute to the formation of school policy
- be professionally committed
- be appropriately self-critical.

This list then serves as a check-list for the teacher undertaking self-assessment.

Critical incidents

Another way of approaching observation is to look for critical incidents in a lesson, selecting three or four happenings which seem to be important for the progress of the lesson and using these as a starting-point for discussion.

Pupil observation

Yet another possibility is to spend some of the time observing a particular pupil or group of pupils and noting what they are doing. Not all the lesson should be spent on this because other things will be missed, but this kind of observation often throws considerable light on the lesson itself.

Observation by senior teachers

This kind of observation of teachers at work involves everyone in a management position in the school in getting to know a great deal about the work of teachers for whom he or she is responsible and this would seem to be valuable.

Observation of the classroom work of departmental staff should be part of the responsibility of every secondary school head of department if he or she is to know how the subject is being taught. Similarly every headteacher of a primary school should be aware of what is happening in the classrooms. Since this observation links with appraisal even when it is undertaken as a normal part of the responsibilities of the headteacher or head of department concerned, it needs to be planned with the appraiser and the teacher concerned. The overall pattern of observation of each teacher's work must be something agreed by the staff of the school as a whole. Topics for discussion should include the pattern of lessons to be observed, establishing beforehand what the teacher is trying to achieve, the form the observation will take, and that discussion of the lesson will take place as soon as possible.

The pattern of lessons to be observed

This needs to be agreed at school level. If the appraiser is to get a fair picture of what happens in the classroom, he or she will need to observe more than one lesson and will need to look at some complete lessons as well as coming in more briefly upon occasion. It was suggested in Chapter 8 that it would be reasonable for at least one of the occasions for visiting to be chosen by the teacher and another by the appraiser. This should give a fair picture of a teacher's work in the classroom.

Establishing what the teacher is trying to achieve

If the appraiser is to make a fair assessment of the teacher's skill in the classroom, it is important to know what the teacher is trying to do so that it can be matched against what actually happens. It is important to be aware of the ways in which observer and the teacher concerned differ in philosophy and make allowances for this. Work should be evaluated in the first place in terms of what the teacher is trying to do, rather than what the observer thinks he or she ought to be doing, although the observer may wish to persuade the teacher to aim at a higher level.

The form the observation will take

Various forms of observation were listed above. The school may decide that everyone will use a similar form of observation and prepare school observation forms. Alternatively a staff may decide that each person observing should be left free to decide for him or herself how the observation should be carried out. There are dangers in this in that the ability to make observations is very varied and some observers will go into the classroom without any plan for observation. This could be to the detriment of the teachers concerned. However, there are also dangers in teachers being aware of the form of observation being undertaken since it is possible to teach to it. It has been shown that teachers being observed tend to ask a larger number of questions, use more praise and make greater play with pupils' answers. See Samph.[77] It may be best to agree that one of a number of forms of observation will be used.

That discussion of the lesson will take place as soon as possible

It is important to discuss what happened as soon as possible after the event so that it is fresh in the memory. The overall impression from several pieces of observation should feed into the appraisal and this will come later.

Ted Wragg[67] suggests the following as possible questions for discussion after observation:

1 What was your own reaction to the lesson? Did it appear to go as planned?
2 In the same circumstances would you do things in the same way? If not, what would you change?
3 How did you feel that the children reacted/behaved in the lesson? Were you satisfied with their contribution and the sort of work they were doing?
4 Was this lesson typical of what usually happens with this class or was it different in any significant way?
5 Will the topic/work be developed in future lessons? If so, how?

Test and examination results

Every secondary school studies examination results to see what can be learned for future reference. Similarly every primary school in LEAs where there is regular testing studies the results. As the National Curriculum and the associated testing become practice there will be more information of this kind available for those conducting teacher appraisal; it is inevitable that it becomes part of the process of considering how well a teacher is doing. However, it is only within the overall context of the school, with people who know the children concerned, that valid judgements can be made about the performance of a group of children and consequently the performance of the teacher.

Study of children's work

Test and examination results are only one aspect of children's performance, however. A head of department in a secondary school or the head of a primary school should be constantly keeping watch on the kind of work which children are producing and on the effectiveness of the teaching they are receiving. It is helpful from time to time to collect in sets of exercise books and to study them. In a primary school where exercise books may not be used for important parts of the work it may be useful to collect in a piece of work from every child occasionally. It can also be valuable to collect a week's work from a small sample of children carefully chosen to represent the most able, the least able and the middle range of a class. This can often be revealing in showing how much or how little has been done.

Written work should not be the only way of checking on children's progress. Discussion with individuals about their work may be useful and it may be helpful to gather a group from time to time and ask for information about what they are doing in some aspect of curriculum. Hearing children read is a common way of checking progress in the early stages of education, though it should be linked with some questioning about each child's understanding of what he or she has read.

Information from pupils

Many teachers are disturbed by the idea that their pupils might be encouraged to make judgements about their teaching. Yet pupils are actually making judgements about teachers all the time and teachers are also using the reaction of pupils to assess their work. Pupils are usually very good judges of teaching and are in the best position of all to make such judgements, since they are the purpose of the exercise. They are also there all the time, whereas observers are there only occasionally.

It is interesting to consider why it is that teachers are worried by the possibility of formalizing this so that the feedback can be used. Teachers are very vulnerable and pupils invited to be critical are likely to have none of the delicacy with which a colleague might deal with the less successful parts of the teacher's work. Too much criticism is damaging to one's self-image; usually pupils, unlike adults, will not separate out the quality of the teaching from the personality of the teacher.

A second reason for not wanting pupils' criticism is that it might disturb the authority relationship of the teacher and make pupils more difficult to work with.

These are both valid reasons for the feeling that pupils should not be invited to comment on their experience in the classroom. Nevertheless it seems a pity not to use such a valuable source of information. It should be possible to devise ways of inviting pupil comment which are helpful rather than threatening by inviting comment on limited questions; in fact most teachers do a good deal of this. For example a teacher might discuss with pupils why something didn't work, inviting them to make suggestions about how it might have been better, perhaps using questions like 'Which bit of that lesson did you think went best?', 'In which bit of the lesson do you think you learned most?' and so on. Discussion about different activities would provide interesting information about ways of organizing work. It might also be interesting to discuss with pupils the way they think they learn best, perhaps as part of a programme on study skills.

Teachers who have a good relationship with the pupils they teach are likely to be offered a good deal of information about pupils' views of what is happening whether they seek it or not. Time spent in exploring some of these comments, perhaps with a small group, may be very helpful.

Another way of getting feedback from pupils is to give them questionnaires from time to time or to invite them to write about work under the headings of 'I enjoyed . . .' and 'I did not enjoy . . .'. Ted Wragg[67] suggests a questionnaire with questions such as

My teacher	
is usually interested in our work	Yes/no
helps slower children in a nice way	Yes/no
tries to be fair to all of us and not to have favourites	Yes/no
explains new work clearly	Yes/no

Each school, in planning appraisal, should consider how the evidence which the pupils have can be drawn out in ways which are non-threatening both to individual teachers and also to the authority relationship which is a necessary part of controlling pupils.

Observation of teacher in a pastoral role

In a secondary school an important part of the work of most teachers is as form tutors; this needs to be taken into account in assessing each teacher's work.

There will normally be someone responsible for form tutors; this may be a year head or a head of house or of a section of the school. These teachers, like the head of department, should be knowledgeable about the form tutors for whom they have responsibility and should try to see them in action in form periods from time to time. Teachers in this role will normally have a good idea of the skill of individual form tutors by the extent to which problems occur. The ability of the individual teacher to manage the administrative part of the form tutor's work will also be evident.

The person responsible for each teacher's appraisal should therefore discuss that teacher's performance as a form tutor with the person responsible for form tutors. It may be that this should be done against an agreed check-list of the responsibilities of the form tutor role or the teacher's job description if the form tutor role appears in it.

In the primary school, the class teacher is responsible both for the pastoral care of children and also for teaching them; these two roles are more or less inseparable. However, some thought should be given in appraisal to whether the teacher is helping the children to develop as individuals, to the extent that the teacher is aware of personal difficulties and problems and is trying to support the children who have them and also to the teacher's ability to cope with the administrative tasks of the job.

Observation of teacher in a management role

In a secondary school, in particular, but also to some extent in a primary school, teachers may occupy management roles and their skill in these roles need to be considered. The list of skills given for self-evaluation may be useful here (see Appendix 1).

Where a teacher is in a management role within the school, it will also be necessary to consider how well he or she is doing in relation to the organization of work within the areas of responsibility; the ability to lead colleagues, drawing together their ideas and developing practice; the ability to support, influence and develop the work of colleagues for whom the teacher is responsible; persistence and skill in liaising with colleagues in complementary roles in feeder and transfer schools; the ability to maintain records and administration; ability to review and evaluate the work within the area of responsibility; persistence and skill in liaising with other teachers in related areas of responsibility; ability to keep up-to-date with recent reports and developments in the area of responsibility and to keep others informed.

Judgements about these skills will be made on a variety of evidence. In some cases it is easy to make a judgement. For example it is easy to pick out the teachers who are good at the administrative aspects of the work and those who are not. Some areas can be judged from the information coming from other people. Teachers in a department where the head of department is very supportive are usually very ready to comment on this and the results of this support are also often evident.

Attendance at meetings led by different teachers will usually provide a good deal of evidence about the ability of the leader to manage adults and lead them forward.

It is easiest to gather evidence for the ability with which any teacher manages a leadership position when there is a clear job description which sets out the responsibilities of the post. It is then possible to seek evidence to match the items in the job description.

Other observation

Most teachers make contributions to the school in addition to teaching. They may run clubs or societies or lead field expeditions. They may make a specific contribution to the discipline structure of the school or liaise with teachers in schools for other phases. Appraisal might also involve a consideration of the regularity with which a teacher has attended appropriate meetings or undertaken in-service opportunities.

Information in all these roles will be available both from observation and from talking with other people. Appraisers are likely to be collecting evidence throughout the year and should also be offering some feedback throughout the year.

Training observers

It cannot be assumed that because someone is a good teacher, he or she will automatically be a good observer. Classroom observation needs training, if only to get some uniformity in what is observed. This can be done in-house by using video tapes and discussing together what is seen. It is also helpful if two people can observe together occasionally so that they can compare notes.

There are various traps which observers can fall into and training may help them to avoid these. They may be inclined to record only negative incidents and give too little attention to what is positive. They may be harder or easier on faults in others which they know they have themselves. They may identify with the teacher to the extent of being critical if the teacher does not do what they would have done in similar circumstances. They may be blinkered in seeing only a limited amount of what is happening because they are mainly interested only in some aspects of what is being observed. They may also miss seeing some things because they lack system.

It is helpful in considering classroom observation to consider what kinds of notes may be helpful in giving feedback to the teacher. Note-making tends to be a rather personal affair and people differ in the kind of note-making which they find helpful. In this context it is important to take very full notes, because they may be used in the future; it is useful to use a carbon pad, so that one copy of the notes can be given to the teacher. The knowledge that a copy of the notes will go to the teacher tends to make the observer note more positive things. It is useful in making notes to note the time at intervals during the lesson so that judgements can be made about the balance of the use of time in the lesson. Note-making from classroom observation should be considered by the staff in making plans for appraisal.

10

Appraisal: the interview

What is involved in the appraisal interview?

The appraisal interview is a key feature of any appraisal system and the skill with which it is managed is crucial to the success of the scheme. It should be a positive experience and a chance for the teacher concerned to talk at some length with a senior colleague, demonstrating the areas of work which he or she feels to be successful. It should also be an opportunity to discuss areas of concern, career possibilities and to agree some plans and goals for the next year. The appraisal interview is also an opportunity for a teacher to say if the management of the work poses problems and to discuss this.

There is a great deal involved in successful appraisal interviewing and it depends in the first place upon the sensitivity with which an appraiser discusses work with his or her colleagues and the trust which has been engendered over the period they have worked together. The appraiser also needs the self-discipline to hold back for much of the time and encourage the teacher to talk. The teacher being appraised should do much more of the talking than the appraiser. This doesn't mean that the teacher should take control of the interview or that the talk should wander. It is the appraiser's task gently to guide the conversation so that important points are discussed, including any which are delicate.

Day, Whitaker and Wren[26] suggest that a teacher asking the question 'What's in it for me?' should be able to answer that question in the following way:

1 I should have a clear understanding of my job and how well I am doing it and what is expected of me.

2 I should feel secure in the knowledge that my talents are known, appreciated and exploited and that my weaknesses have been identified and constructive help has been offered to improve them.

3 I should have discussed my future, including my ambitions and career prospects, and have received guidance in achieving these ambitions.

4 I should feel satisfied that all aspects of my work in and around the school have been discussed in a professional way.

5 I should feel happy that everything discussed will be treated in confidence and any written note will be owned by myself and my interviewer alone.

Venue

The place where an appraisal interview is held is important. The two people concerned need to be comfortable and undisturbed for the period of the interview. They need to sit facing each other so that each can clearly see the other's face; neither should be against the light. If possible the situation in which one participant sits behind a desk should be avoided, since the desk can act as a barrier to exchange as well as physically.

Schools will need to see that this kind of venue can be made available for interviews at regular intervals.

Preparing for the interview

Both parties to an appraisal interview need to prepare for it and it is helpful if preparation requirements are discussed and agreed by the staff generally.

The appraiser needs to assemble the information for discussion. This may include records of all the information discussed in Chapter 9, together with any other material which seems to be relevant. A copy of the teacher's job description will be needed and information from any previous appraisal interview.

The *Report of the Consortium of School Teacher Appraisal Pilot Schemes*[66] suggests that the appraiser's preparation should involve the following:

1 consulting the teacher's factual profile and previous summary
2 consulting with the support teacher (if one exists) and reviewing the summary
3 consulting with other colleagues who have responsibility for aspects of the teacher's performance
4 reflection on the teacher's performance over the past period and the teacher's individual preparation form for the meeting.

To this might be added 'studying the reports of classroom observation'.

An appropriate form will be needed to support self-appraisal on the part of the teacher. A suggested form is given in Appendix 1 but there are many others available. In particular, the Suffolk publication *In the Light of Torches*[73] provides a variety of forms and check-lists. Suffolk Education Department has also published three papers under the title *Teacher Appraisal: A Practical Guide*[72] of which Part 3 is concerned entirely with documents. A number of schools also ask teachers to contribute annually to their records a statement of the group(s) taught that year, the broad areas of work covered and any other contributions to the life of the school. This provides useful information for the appraisal interview and also ensures that the headteacher has up-to-date information about anyone for whom a confidential report needs to be written.

The stages of an appraisal interview

Opening the interview

The opening of an appraisal interview is very important. It sets the scene and may determine the climate of the interview. It is a prerequisite of a successful appraisal interview that both people are relaxed enough to concentrate on the matter in hand and to talk frankly. In arranging for an appraisal interview everything possible should be done to avoid interruptions, distractions and discomfort so that both participants can concentrate on the task in hand.

There are five tasks to be done in the opening part of the interview. These will be important the first time a person conducts an appraisal interview. They will be less important when the teacher being interviewed knows what to expect, but the appraiser may still need to take some account of them.

The appraiser should put the interviewee at ease

There are various ways of doing this. It helps to start by chatting informally about general topics over a cup of coffee. It may be useful to ask about the other person's family or hobbies or to talk fairly generally about work. It is helpful, if possible, to find some topic which is non-threatening on which the other person can talk easily. This discussion should be fairly brief.

The form of the interview should be explained

Suggestions about the form of the interview are outlined below. The appraiser should stress that although he or she has a pattern in mind, the interview can be flexible to suit the needs of the other person.

The teacher should be asked what he or she wishes to get from the interview

The appraisal interview is for the benefit of both parties. It is important that the person being appraised feels that his or her needs are being taken into account.

The structure of the interview should be agreed

When it is clear what the other person wishes to get from the interview and the appraiser has described the way he or she has planned it, teacher and appraiser can agree on the way it will go.

The appraiser should describe his or her role

Anticipation of an appraisal interview can be threatening. It is therefore important to establish that the exercise is intended to be constructive and of value to the other person and should be the outcome of his or her preparation. The appraiser's role involves reflecting performance and talking through problems and subsequently trying to support any development which has been agreed.

The body of the interview

During the body of the interview there are eight main points to bear in mind.

The agreed plan should be used flexibly

The agreed structure is simply a framework for discussion. The appraiser should be prepared to move away from it if there is something interesting which seems to need discussion, but still keeping the overall plan in mind.

The appraiser's task is to get the other person to talk about work, plans, ideas and feelings

We have already noted that the person being appraised should do the majority of the talking during the interview, but may need the appraiser's encouragement to talk freely.

The appraiser should listen carefully, respond and extend what is said by questioning

Some of the forms of response and questioning that are possible are analysed on pp. 158–64. An appraiser should try to select responses and questions which will move the discussion forward in the direction of helping the other person to think through issues and problems which concern him or her. If possible the appraiser should lead the teacher towards working out his or her own solutions to such issues and problems, rather than offering ready-made ideas although there is also a place for making suggestions. There may also be situations where the appraiser wishes to lead the teacher in the direction of developments which will achieve school aims.

The appraiser needs to select carefully opportunities to make
critical statements if any are needed

The appraisal interview offers a good opportunity to place criticism in a supportive and positive context and to work to build confidence before getting to issues of concern. It is important for the appraiser to state what he or she has to say clearly and unambiguously. This is dealt with in greater detail on pp. 168–9.

The appraiser should summarize at intervals

This gives the appraiser the opportunity to check that he or she is getting the right picture and move the discussion on. The appraiser also needs to ensure that the other person is accepting what is being said. The points to be accepted need to be selected carefully when a section of the discussion comes to an end and moves on to a different topic.

Development and career prospects should be discussed
as part of the interview

When development is being discussed, the ways in which the everyday life of the school can contribute should be considered as well as more formal in-service opportunities. (Ways of doing this were discussed in Chapter 2.) This discussion should result in a plan for each person which identifies the particular ways in which development might take place. It is important to avoid raising false hopes of promotion. It is better to be honest with someone who is unlikely to achieve further promotion and to seek instead to find forms of job enrichment which may help to keep the teacher working happily.

Goals should be agreed

These will be part of the planning which the teacher will attempt during the course of the next year or so. Goal-setting is dealt with in greater detail on pp. 166–8.

Comment about any problems should be invited

Some problems will appear to teachers to arise because of the way the school runs and this may be an opportunity to identify these. Appraisal is a two-way process and teachers may often have comments which are useful for management to hear. They need to be invited to make such comments.

Closing the interview

A person will go away from an appraisal interview with what happened at the end very fresh in his or her mind. It is therefore important that this should in some sense summarize the whole exercise and that the ending should be positive. The following six points may be part of the closing of the interview.

The appraiser should check that both parties have covered their plans

If the plan has been worked through in a fairly flexible way there may be sections left at the end which need to be covered. It is important to check this.

A check should be made to see that the teacher feels that the ground has been covered

It is important that the teacher also feels that everything he or she wishes to discuss has been considered.

It may be necessary to return to some points

The appraiser may have noted points as the interview proceeded which required further consideration or some earlier points may need to be re-emphasized.

Progress and achievement should be summarized

The appraisal interview offers an opportunity for a formal recognition of achievement. The interview should end on a positive note with genuine praise.

Plans on both sides should be reviewed

In the process of going through the interview some goals will have been agreed and some plans arrived at both for the teacher and for the appraiser: these need to be summarized.

Arrangements for reporting should be reviewed

Some of the plans made should have a time-scale and will therefore need to be checked at appropriate intervals. There should be agreement as to how this will be done.

Skills involved in appraisal interviewing

Some of the skills involved in interviewing include the following, which we shall discuss in detail below.

1 Listening and body language
2 Questioning
3 Responding
4 Summarizing
5 Problem-solving
6 Goal-setting
7 Being direct
8 Counselling.

Listening and body language

Listening is a very important part of the appraisal process. It is not a passive activity but one in which the listener needs to be alert not only to the things the other person is saying but also to the messages about feelings and perceptions which may underlie the words and to body language. People are continually sending messages which tell how they are reacting to a situation. An appraiser needs to be able to read these. It must also be remembered that people will often disguise the real nature of a sensitive problem by talking about a much simpler problem. The appraiser needs to be aware of the following six points.

Eye contact

Eye contact is an essential element in interpersonal exchange. In conversation people normally make eye contact when they start to say something and look down or away as they finish. Eye contact is important in retaining trust. 'He won't look you in the eye' is a common expression implying lack of trust.

Interest, involvement and concern

People signal that they are listening and are interested by eye contact, smiles, nods, sounds of agreement, etc. Signals of this kind demonstrate to the speaker that the listener is actually listening.

Tension

A listener needs to be conscious of tension in others. People demonstrate that they are tense by the way they sit, which may look uncomfortable. They may clench/unclench their hands, wind their legs around the chair, demonstrate tension in tight facial muscles, by frowning or by showing a dry mouth or in a number of other ways. An appraiser needs to do everything possible to help the other person to relax.

Lack of interest, impatience or boredom

People signal lack of interest by losing eye contact or by fidgeting; playing with something; sitting back and looking far away; looking at a watch or the clock, and so on. Impatience is usually signalled by fidgeting. A listener needs to be careful not to exhibit any of these signs and to be aware of them in the other person. People also tend to fidget when the conversation is making them uncomfortable.

Emotional involvement

In the course of a meeting the situation may become emotionally charged. An appraiser may wish to move away from a delicate subject or to press it as tactfully as possible in order to ensure that the point has been fully made and then try to be supportive.

Views of relative status

People are not always conscious of the way in which others convey messages about their views of relative status. The senior person in an interview normally exercises a degree of control over what happens. It is easy for the person in this position to talk too much and do too little listening.

It is also easy to use status to dismiss or encourage other people's ideas; a headteacher is in a particularly powerful position for doing this. Headteachers tend to speak with greater confidence and authority than other people and may hold eye contact until the other person drops it.

People who see themselves in more junior positions will reverse these actions. They will back down easily if the senior partner appears to be unsympathetic. They may put ideas forward tentatively and apologetically and it may be the responsibility of the senior person to draw them out so that they are able to make a contribution.

A person in a senior position also needs to be aware that people will be careful in what they say to him or her. It is important to question to get behind some of the things which people say.

Problems with listening

The following things may go wrong with listening. The listener may

- hear only what he or she wants to hear
- be too concerned with what he or she is going to say next to listen properly to the other person
- have other things on his or her mind and find it difficult to concentrate on the speaker
- be in a hurry and appear to listen on the run.

Questioning

Questioning is an important part of the appraisal interview. If the appraiser is to be effective in helping teachers to consider their performance, he or she needs to be a skilled questioner. This means asking the right questions at the right time. Skilful questioning can contribute to problem-solving by

1 establishing facts
2 eliciting feelings
3 getting the other person involved
4 checking understanding
5 stimulating thought
6 enabling agreement
7 bringing attention back to the issue in hand.

Questions can be of different types: open, closed and variations of these.

Open questions

These are non-directive and may be used to draw out a wide range of responses encouraging the other person to talk freely.

Most open questions cannot be answered with a simple yes or no. They often begin with 'What', 'How', or 'Why' and do not lead in a specific direction. They encourage the other person to elaborate on objectives, needs, wants, problems and the current situation. They should help to draw out the other person's feelings and opinions help him or her to discover things and think out ideas.

Examples of open questions
● What do you think of that idea?
● How could we handle this curriculum change?
● What might help you to improve in that area?
● Why do you think you're having difficulty with this?

Closed questions

These are directive; they restrict the person to a narrow range of answers because the query is more specific. Closed questions usually establish facts and allow specific information to be obtained. They tend to direct a discussion to a specific area and can help to reinforce points and avoid misunderstandings. They allow a particular area to be probed and make it difficult for the person replying to evade the point.

Examples of closed questions
● Do you think this should be changed?
● How many times has this happened in the last month?
● When will you finish this?
● Is this your major priority?

Variations on open and closed questions

Fact-finding questions	'How long will this take you?'
Feeling-finding questions	'Are you happy with this idea?'
Clarifying questions	'Are you referring to someone in your department?'
Developmental questions	'Can you explain a bit further about that?'
Directing questions	'You said you had a couple of ideas – what was the other one?'
Testing questions	'Do you think you can cope?'
Closing questions	'What are you going to do next?

Points to remember

The right question should be used at the right time. Closed questions should be avoided when trying to develop confidence and openness in an individual. It is usually best to move from open questions to narrower, more probing ones, picking up on information given in the initial stages.

The other person needs time to consider and structure his or her response to questions. It is important not to jump in with another question unless the other person seems to be in real difficulties, in which case the appraiser may want to break down the original questions into a series of less demanding questions.

A broad plan of the areas to be covered should be prepared. This should not be too precise and some thought should be given to the kinds of questions which will elicit appropriate responses. This helps in getting started and also helps the appraiser to check that nothing has been missed.

Responses should be developed as they come. The appraiser should concentrate on listening to – and watching – the way the other person responds to each question. Subsequent questions can then be framed from the previous response, perhaps probing into what was said or asking questions to extend it. Each area should either be explored fully at the time it is raised or a note should be made to return to it at a later stage.

One main area should be covered at a time. The appraiser should avoid flitting from one area to another and while remaining flexible should be careful not to get distracted from the main theme of the discussion.

The types of questions used should be mixed, with the balance in favour of open questions.

Responding

The way in which an appraiser responds to the statements a person makes affects the outcome of discussion. In general it is important to be positive and encouraging in responding and to make the other person feel that his or her work and progress is important. The way the appraiser responds not only shows whether the appraiser has been listening carefully to what the teacher has been saying, but also demonstrates to the other person the extent to which the appraiser is sensitive to the way the teacher is feeling about what is being discussed.

Responses can be classified in various ways: one useful classification is evaluative, interpretative, supportive, probing and understanding types of responses.

Evaluative response

Evaluative responses tend either to be judgemental or to offer advice. The appraiser may indicate approval or disapproval of what the other person says or does and there may be an implication that he or she has made a judgement about the appropriateness, effectiveness or rightness of what the other person has said. Evaluative responses often involve offering solutions to problems or commenting on what should or should not be done.

It was noted earlier that it is normally better to lead people through to their own solutions to problems than to offer them ready-made. However, it would seem to be appropriate for the appraiser to indicate his or her own values or views when the other person asks directly for the appraiser's opinion. A teacher may also want advice or positive suggestions when he or she is not able to offer personal solutions to a particular situation.

There are dangers in using evaluative responses too frequently. When people feel they are being criticized they are likely to feel inhibited; they are less likely to open up and offer honest ideas and feelings. If an appraiser frequently offers solutions to another person's problems, they may become dependent and start to rely on being given a solution rather than seeking their own. If solutions are offered too quickly, before the problem has been identified and agreed, it may be unsuitable.

Interpretative response

A person who makes an interpretative response will be trying to read between the lines and interpret what the other person is saying. He or she is likely to be saying things like 'What you really mean is . . .'. It may involve teaching or imparting meaning to the other person by seeing links or sensing messages which he or she may not be aware of.

Interpretative responses may help the other person to see the hitherto hidden implications in what he or she says. For example 'When you say you enjoy teaching the able pupils in your classes, are you also saying that you dislike teaching the less able?' An interpretative style can often help to break through conscious or unconscious defence mechanisms. For example 'You keep saying you're not ambitious. I think you're really saying that you are ambitious and are frustrated because you haven't yet succeeded in getting promotion.'

In reflecting back what the other person is saying with interpretations there is the danger that the appraiser may be seen as not listening properly or lacking in interest: this may produce or increase inhibitions, mistrust or annoyance. There is also the problem that if the interpretations are incorrect the other person may find it difficult to say so honestly and misunderstanding will follow.

Supportive response

This style is used when the appraiser wishes to give reassurance or pacify the other person. The intention is to reduce the other person's negative feelings such as anger or depression and increase his or her esteem and confidence. Supportive responses are those which offer psychological support. Typical examples might be as follows:

- 'That really is a good idea.'
- 'You mustn't worry too much over this.'
- 'I can understand how it happened.'
- 'Of course you can do the job – I have every confidence in you.'

Supportive statements can be very encouraging, can raise self-esteem and can increase confidence and enthusiasm. When an appraiser makes a supportive statement after the other person has suggested a good solution to his or her own problem it endorses the behaviour and reinforces it for the future.

On the other hand, supportive statements do not move the discussion on beyond giving psychological support. Too many supportive statements can lead to blocking discussion of a problem – particularly when the other person has a genuine problem. A person who favours the supportive style may find it difficult to confront a deficiency in someone else for fear of hurting feelings or undermining confidence.

Probing response

An appraiser uses a probing style in order to gather further information, explore the other person's ideas, perceptions or feelings. This style is characterized by open questions which include words like:

- 'Why...?'
- 'How...?'
- 'Where...?'
- 'What...?'
- 'When...?'
- 'Who...?'
- 'Tell me more about...?'

e.g. 'Could you tell me more about the idea you have for developing a new scheme of work for the fourth year?'

'Why do you think that happened?'
'What should we do about that?'
'How do you feel about it?'

A probing style can be used to achieve two objectives. It can help the appraiser to build up a better picture of the situation. It can also be used to help the other person to explore the situation. A series of probing questions can help someone to clarify a problem, explore facts not previously considered important or express feelings about a problem.

Probing responses are useful in ensuring that a situation is fully explored before working on what to do about it. Such responses can often help a person to reach insights which he or she wouldn't have achieved alone. They ensure that individuals think through the situation for themselves.

On the other hand, continued probing and questioning can be seen as threatening and can inhibit. It is also possible to go on collecting information and exploring the situation with probing questions for too long and not get round to exploring what should be done.

Understanding response

An understanding response is non-directive and non-evaluative. It is used when the appraiser wants to check that he or she has a correct understanding of what the other person is saying and how he or she feels and sees the situation. To do this the appraiser reflects back what the other person is saying or feeling in an empathetic way.

e.g. 'You seem to feel frustrated about that.'
       'You obviously feel strongly about that.'
       'As I understand it, what you are saying is . . .'

The process of checking understanding ensures that the interviewer really has heard and understood what the other person is saying. Understanding responses deal effectively with other people's feelings by referring to them and allowing open discussion about them. They also allow the other person to express his or her perception of the situation fully without fear of judgement or contradiction.

The extent to which this type of response is used should be limited, however. Continued reflecting back can be frustrating for the other person by sounding parrot-like. An understanding response does not in itself move the discussion on.

Which response to use

Most people have a style of response which is more habitual to them than the others, over-using some categories and under-using others. The most frequently used response tends to be in the evaluative style. There is no best style. Each type of response has its advantages and disadvantages and may be effective in some situations but ineffective in others. A good appraiser will have the ability and the sensitivity to use the whole repertoire of responses appropriately in a given situation.

Summarizing

It was noted earlier that it is important for the interviewer to summarize at intervals. The process of noting the important points and seeing how they fit together at the same time as listening intently is not an easy one. Most people need to take notes during an appraisal interview and it may be a good idea for the appraiser to explain to the teacher concerned that these are purely for his or her own information in order to remember what the teacher was saying.

There are many different ways of taking notes, but it may be hepful, when taking notes in an appraisal interview, to note points on different parts of the page and link them together with lines and arrows or by circling them. This makes the summarizing process easier because pieces of information which belong together can be physically linked with a line or they can be numbered to create an appropriate order.

Summarizing is really a way of checking that the record is a correct one and of giving the other person a chance to check. As the interview continues it becomes a way of leading into possible targets and identifying particular problems to be solved.

Problem-solving

Most appraisal interviews will give rise to some problems which need to be solved. There are many ways of tackling problem-solving but the following stages are nearly always needed:

Define the problem

It is useful to start by trying to state the problem clearly, perhaps defining the situation as it is now and the situation which is desirable.

Analyse the problem

It is then helpful to talk round the problem, looking at different aspects of it and trying to see it from different points of view. This discussion should take into account how the teacher concerned and possibly other people feel about it. People's emotional attitudes towards a problem may make it impossible to apply a straightforward and logical solution. This discussion may lead to a redefinition of the problem.

There are some techniques which are useful at this stage. One of these is Kurt

Figure 9   Force field analysis

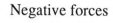

Negative forces

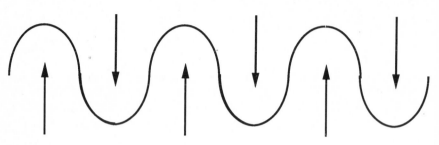

Positive forces

Lewin's[78] force field analysis (see Figure 9). This is based on the idea that any situation is a balance between restraining forces and driving forces. By making a list of the restraining forces in a particular situation and the driving forces which work in favour of the desired change it becomes possible to see some of the aspects of the problem which are relevant to its solution. The task is then to see what actions could be taken to reduce or eliminate the restraining forces and what actions could be taken to increase the driving forces. Another approach is described in K. F. Jackson's *The Art of Solving Problems.*[79] He suggests listing the obstacles in the way of getting from the present state of the problem to the desired state. He then suggests considering each in turn and looking at whether any of the following approaches might work:

1 overcome it
2 go round it
3 remove it
4 demolish it
5 neutralize it
6 prove it to be illusory
7 turn it to advantage
8 buy it off
9 alter it
10 find its weakest point
11 wait for it to go away

Generate solutions

It is very easy to think of one solution and seize on it. At this stage it is better to try to think of as many solutions as possible, including some which are unlikely. This thinking then provides a basis for selecting a good solution.

It is important to allow the teacher concerned to come up with solutions, although the appraiser may offer some also. The appraiser should avoid biasing the discussion towards solutions which have worked for him or her. They may not work for the teacher concerned, who has to make the solutions selected his or her own.

Select a solution

The ideas which have been discussed can now be considered as possibilities. Some will be rejected immediately; others will need discussion until one gradually comes to the fore.

Goal-setting

The process of appraisal involves agreeing some goals or targets. These are one-off, specific improvements or developments which are singled out for special attention, something to achieve over and above normal work. Goal-setting provides, on the one hand, the opportunity for the teacher to identify something he or she wants to achieve and, on the other hand, an opportunity for the appraiser to encourage teachers towards goals which contribute to school or departmental goals. Goals should not be allowed to distort the rest of the job, which still has to be carried out to a high standard. The way in which goals are defined and the part which goal-setting plays in appraisal may differ from one school to another and according to the preferences of those concerned, but the process implies agreeing targets. Goals should be designed to stretch the person involved. Three or four goals per year is sufficient; there should be the opportunity to redefine goals if circumstances change.

Goals are only part of the job

The goals which are agreed concern selected parts of the job. They reflect the emphasis which an individual wishes to put on a particular part of the job at a given time. They are concerned with improvement or development in a particular area.

Goals may be related to the job description

Each teacher should have a job description in which it is possible to see that each part is being achieved and discussion of this may be part of the appraisal interview. Goals may be agreed in a given year suggesting that the teacher will work particularly to improve performance in one part of the job description.

Goals may be related to the aims a teacher is currently pursuing

At any given time a teacher may wish to pursue certain aims in his or her work: the teachers' goals in a particular year may be related to these. Thus one goal in the first year of service in a school might be to get to know the staff and children and assess their needs in the area for which the teacher has responsibility. In the following year the teacher may be concerned with some kind of change, perhaps developing and introducing a new scheme of work or helping children to develop work from first-hand experience. The teacher with responsibilities for other teachers may be concerned to develop particular ways of working with colleagues or to improve the work in a particular aspect of curriculum in certain ways.

Goals should be linked to the aims of the school and year
or department

Individual goals should reflect the goals the school or section of the school is pursuing.

Goals should be stated in a form which enables those concerned
to see that they have been achieved

In setting goals it is important to remember that it will be necessary later to assess how far they have been achieved. This means that they need to be definite enough for this to be possible. A vague statement such as 'Improve record-keeping' is useful only if what will be regarded as improvement is defined. What is needed is a statement such as 'Maintain a weekly record of progress of all the pupils I teach'. Where possible and relevant there should also be a statement of performance criteria. In the example given above we might add 'with at least one entry made for each pupil' (this might not be a realistic aim for some teachers in a secondary school, but would be appropriate in a primary school).

Goals should be limited in number

The number of goals which any individual takes on should be limited to what is possible. Three goals is normally enough for one individual.

Goals should be time-bonded

The achievement of a goal should be within a defined period. Periods for achieving goals may vary and the appraiser will need to agree dates with the teacher by which each goal will be achieved.

Strategies for achieving goals should be discussed

How goals are to be achieved should be considered. Detailed plans for each goal should be discussed so that it is clear that the teacher concerned will be able to do what is being planned. Any financial implications should be carefully considered.

Progress towards goals should be monitored at suitable intervals

It is part of the task of the appraiser to monitor progress towards goals. This will be a matter of brief discussion from time to time to see how things are going and agreeing modification or redefinition if circumstances have changed. The appraiser ought also to keep a note of the completion date of all goals and check that they have been achieved.

The ability to set appropriate goals takes time to develop. Trethowan[18] suggests that teachers need to develop their skills as target-setters to the point where the following criteria are true.

1 They want to be responsible for setting their own targets.
2 They are interested and can select important target areas.
3 They identify with the aims and ethos of the school.
4 They know how to set targets and how to deal with the problems which can arise from them.
5 They have sufficient maturity to adjust targets when necessary.

Being direct

There is often a need in appraisal to tell someone that something is wrong or not good enough. This is not an easy thing to do, but appraisal offers a good context for doing it. If the appraisal is well conducted there is a long enough period to discuss positive as well as negative points and to allow the other person to talk through problems.

Where a teacher is not doing well, the appraiser should first try to discover the nature of the problem, both in preparation for the interview and in discussion during the interview, when he or she can seek to discover how the teacher views the problem. The difficulty could be (among other things):

1 lack of subject knowledge
2 lack of teaching knowledge/skill
3 lack of skill in organizing work
4 inability to relate to pupils
5 lack of skill in managing pupils
6 inability to match work to pupils
7 inability to relate to colleagues
8 personal problems
9 illness
10 stress
11 lack of challenge
12 the working environment.

The appraiser has the task of tackling the problem directly. The following points should be considered.

The timing within the interview for tackling the task should be carefully chosen

The interview should deal with some of the more positive things first and to create the kind of atmosphere which makes it possible to discuss the problem.

The interviewee should be led towards the problem by questioning

The ideal is for the person being appraised to formulate the problem rather than the appraiser. This makes it very much easier to deal with.

The problem should be stated or re-stated clearly

If the other person actually formulates the problem, the appraiser may simply need to re-state it. If he or she does not come near to stating it the appraiser will then need to spell it out very clearly, without pulling any punches. The appraiser should try to retain eye contact in doing this, because this will give information about how the other person is reacting. It also makes it clear that what the appraiser is saying applies to him or her.

The appraiser should try to persuade the teacher to accept what is being said

It is important that the other person really understands and, if possible, accepts what the appraiser is saying. This may mean repeating the statement in various ways until it seems to be accepted. This is not always easy and the appraiser may have to settle for less than full acceptance of the statement. In this situation it is often helpful to go on to the next stage.

There should be a positive discussion of what can be done

The interview then becomes a problem-solving session. The appraiser should be very supportive over this, exploring as many avenues as possible.

Appraiser and teacher together should identify steps which can actually be taken

They should try to find a number of things which can easily be done to help the problem, both by the person concerned and by others. This should be built into a programme with a time-scale and a monitoring process. This may be part of the teacher's goal-setting programme.

Counselling

A good deal of the work that a good appraiser does involves a form of counselling, although counselling in the context of appraisal may not provide the same measure of detachment on the part of the appraiser that would be expected in counselling in some other contexts where the counsellor has no vested interest in the outcome. Carl Rogers[80] suggested that three qualities were needed in a counsellor – empathy, warmth and genuineness. He believes that for counselling to be effective, the counsellor must communicate in an open and direct way with the client so that the client feels able to disclose his or her concerns and problems and be open to the possibilities of change. There should be an element of this in a good appraisal interview, although the normal status relationship between the two people cannot and should not be set aside.

Francesca Inskipp[81] defines counselling as follows:

1 Providing help and support for someone who is concerned or perplexed.
2 Creating a safe and accepting climate so that the other person can talk freely and openly about problems and their associated feelings.
3 Helping the other person to gain insight into problems so as to generate practical solutions to them.

Stenning and Stenning[82] suggest that there are three common failings in appraisal interviews:

1 The activity fails to secure the commitment of the participants 'largely because appraisers lack adequate training and convey that they begrudge the time it takes to carry out the procedure'.
2 There are threats to objectivity such as the halo effect, stereotyping and others.
3 Some schemes degenerate into 'going through the motions' because 'little attempt may be made to incorporate assessments into any corporate or individual framework'.

A further point to be borne in mind is that appraiser and appraisee have to go on living and working together. If the appraisal interview is threatening, it will be a threat to the future work of the people concerned.

Meyer[83] records a number of findings of experience with appraisal in the General Electric Company in the 1960s. Although this is a long time ago and records information in an industrial rather than a school setting, the findings are still relevant for schools.

1 Criticism has a negative effect upon the achievement of goals.
2 Performance improves most when specific goals are established.
3 Defensiveness resulting from critical appraisal produces inferior performance.
4 Coaching should be a day-to-day, not a once-a-year, activity.
5 Mutual goal-setting, not criticism, improves performance.

6 Interviews designed primarily to improve people's performance should not at the same time weigh their salary or promotion in the balance.
7 Participation by the employee in the goal-setting process helps to produce favourable results.

Gill[84] suggests that success in appraisal interviews is associated with

1 a high level of subordinate participation in the appraisal process
2 a helpful and constructive attitude on the part of the appraiser (as opposed to a critical one)
3 a problem-solving approach by the interviewer (as opposed to a 'tell and sell' style)
4 participation by the employee in setting any specific goals to be achieved.

None of this means that the appraiser should avoid critical comment, but that it should be undertaken in a constructive way, seeking solutions to a problem rather than apportioning blame. Problems need to be analysed in a positive way, looking for steps which could be taken to overcome them and encouraging the other person to take a positive approach.

Recording the interview

The last stage of the appraisal interview is the provision of a record. It is now laid down that:

> the appraiser, in consultation with the appraisee, shall prepare an appraisal statement recording the main points made in the discussion and the conclusions reached, including targets.

This does not preclude the recording of any point of disagreement. A suggested form of recording is given in Appendix 3 and there are numerous suggestions in the literature, particularly in the Suffolk Education Department's booklet *Teacher Appraisal: A Practical Guide, Part 3.*[72]

The appraiser will have the notes taken during the interview, together with any notes taken from classroom observation and the teacher's own preparation material. These provide material for the body of the report.

The most usual way of recording appraisal interviews is to use a standard form so that similar information is recorded about each person. There are at least two possible approaches to forms of reporting, both of which would seem possible within the regulations.

First, the appraiser can agree what is recorded with the teacher concerned and both sign the record. This means that they must agree what they are going to put, particularly about points of disagreement. This can make the record something of a compromise.

Second, the appraiser can record what he or she feels is important and then invite the teacher to add comments about any points of disagreement before signing it.

It is now a requirement that the goals for each person be recorded separately so that they can be given to the chairman of governors if he or she requests to see them.

Following-up appraisal

Each appraisal interview should end with discussion about the teacher's development and with a plan for this which includes opportunities within the everyday life of the school as well as in-service opportunities. There is a requirement for a further meeting after a year and there may also be a need for further brief meetings to discuss the way the plan is going and progress towards goals. It should in any case be part of the appraiser's normal work to follow-up appraisal and support the work of the teachers for whom he or she is responsible.

11

Teacher records

The contents of teachers' files

The records a school keeps of the work of its staff are an important part of the professional development plan and should be used in considering the development of each individual.

A teacher's file may contain material of various kinds. Some of the material will be permanent or semi-permanent, e.g. information about appointment, salary, grading, and so on. Other material will be relevant for a period only, e.g. letters or other written material from or about the teacher. The easiest way to keep these separate is to use plastic files, possibly of different colours, for each of the semi-permanent topics and to leave temporary material loose in the file. If a coloured sheet is inserted in each file each summer, it becomes easy to remove outdated material after a given period, possibly two years.

The material within the file should include sub-files on the teacher's appointment and service material, together with records of work undertaken, in-service training and appraisals.

Appointment and service material

This includes the original particulars of the post and the application form, together with notes made at the time of appointment. (It is a good idea to make a note at the time of appointment of the impression made by the successful candidate and his or her possible potential. This can then be used later to assess how good was the judgement made at the time.)

This file should also include the letter of appointment or contract which gives details of the post and the salary, and a note of any promotion or allowances given.

Record of work undertaken

There should be a record, preferably prepared annually by the teacher, probably at the time of his or her appraisal interview, which gives information about the group(s) taught, any pastoral work, contributions to the life of the school, responsibilities undertaken, membership of committees and working parties, contribution to extra-curricular activities and anything else which seems relevant.

This record provides valuable information for the appraisal interview and for writing a report if the teacher applies for another post. It can also be studied in considering the way a teacher's work might develop. For example it will be helpful in a primary school to have a record of the groups a teacher has taken so that experience can be widened by taking a different group. In a secondary school there may be development in widening the ability range of groups taught or giving more experience as a form tutor. At all levels it will be clear whether a teacher has had good opportunities of taking responsibility.

Record of in-service training

The simplest way of keeping this record is to use evaluation sheets completed by any teacher who attends a course, inside or outside the school. As it is helpful to other people if these sheets are kept in a file in the staffroom for reference, it will be necessary to make a copy for the teacher's own file.

This sub-file may also include an annual statement of the teacher's development plan, which has emerged from appraisal and from discussion with the professional development co-ordinator.

Appraisal record

This file may include the preparation form and record of appraisal. It may also contain the notes on classroom observation. It should contain a clear statement of the goals agreed.

Confidentiality

Files of this kind will contain much that should be confidential to the headteacher and the teacher concerned, although some sections of it may need to be made available to the person who does a teacher's appraisal. This is a good reason for having a number of sub-files within the file overall. An appraiser can easily be given the files on the records of work undertaken, in-service training and appraisal.

Teachers must have confidence that only the headteacher will have access to their files. Confidentiality must be seen to be observed. Staff files need to be kept where there is little chance of unlawful access and they should be kept locked at all times. The key should probably be kept by the headteacher or at least by a senior secretary who is very conscious of the confidential nature of the material and aware that no one should be given the key. Teachers requiring sub-files for appraisal should be given them only by the headteacher or by the designated senior secretary.

12
In-service providers

The school in-service programme should not only make use of opportunities for teachers to attend outside courses, but also consider whether the various in-service providers in the neighbourhood can offer what the school requires. This will to some extent be governed by the cost of the provision, but some provision, for example that offered by the advisory services, may well be free. Most of the local providers are likely to be offering courses of their own designing, perhaps at the instigation of the local authority, and teachers may well wish to make use of these but most of them will also be prepared to provide courses or other in-service activities to meet the needs of individual schools or groups of schools.

Providers who might contribute

Higher education staff

Staff from a university, college of education or polytechnic might contribute. Some good examples of the sort of contribution which might be made are given in *In-Service, the Teacher and the School*[85] edited by Carol Donoughue and in *School Focused Staff Development*[86] by Eric Hewton.

Lectures

A lecture based on the research findings in a particular area of work may be very helpful if this is an area in which the school is especially interested. When studying some part of the school's work the teachers concerned may wish to have an academic input at an early stage.

Courses leading to a certificate, diploma or degree

These might be based at the school or at the college concerned. Quite a number of certificates, diplomas and degrees now link in closely with the work being done by a teacher in school and there is often good opportunity to negotiate aspects of the work so that it helps to meet school goals as well as leading to a qualification for the teacher.

Consultancy over particular aspects of the school's work

Higher education staff are often in a position to analyse what is happening and do not pose any threat to teachers since they have no responsibility for the work of the school. College of education staff may also be able to involve students in observation. In one primary school, for example, a team teaching organization was not going well. The local college brought a group of students, each of whom observed what a particular child was doing. As a result of this study, the teachers were able, successfully, to alter their way of working to take into account the findings of the study.

Evaluation

Higher education staff are able to offer both to evaluate particular aspects of the school's work or of the professional development programme and may also be able to help to train the school staff in evaluation techniques.

Action research

Higher education staff may be able to work with groups of teachers helping them to develop the skills to undertake action research within the school.

Classroom observation

College of education staff need to be expert in classroom observation. They may be able to help when the staff is developing the skills of classroom observation for appraisal.

Exchange arrangements and involvement of students

College of education staff need to spend time teaching in schools and this may be arranged so that the teachers released can undertake professional development activity. The involvement of teaching students may also make some activities in school possible by ensuring that there are more adults about.

Problems in using higher education staff

There are certain problems which schools may encounter in working with higher education staff. There may be a certain credibility gap between the classroom practitioner and the higher education teacher, which only experience of higher education staff working in schools can bridge. There is also the problem that some higher education teachers are better than others. The negotiation involved in getting the right person can be somewhat delicate. The cost of higher education staff may also be prohibitive if a school plans to use their services extensively.

Advisers and inspectors

It is the task of the advisory service to provide support and help for teachers in the classroom and support and help to the school as a whole. It is also the task of the service to inspect schools and offer advice accordingly, to offer subject and school management advice and to provide in-service courses for teachers, although most services are now coming to recognize that they must be organizers of in-service courses rather than contributors to them. In addition most advisers spend a good deal of time advising governors on selection interviewing.

Advice on practice

Advisers should be able to advise headteachers and teachers on ways of working, on equipment and materials for particular purposes. They should be able to offer experience of other schools in working in particular ways or with particular materials. Advisers should also be able to analyse practice and identify where problems are occurring.

Advice on organization and management

Someone within the advisory service should be able to advise headteachers and other senior staff on the way the school is organized and on alternative possibilities.

Advice on forms of in-service provision for school-based work

Advisers should have ideas about the way in which a school could provide training for particular purposes and the kinds of activities likely to achieve the desired ends.

A contribution to an in-service programme

Advisers should have many possible contributions to make to a school's in-service programme, both as lecturers and as leaders of activities.

Problems in using advisers

The major problem about using advisers is that they are very pressed for time and it may be difficult to persuade a particular adviser to give time to an individual school's in-service programme. They may also be seen as creating an element of threat for teachers, because of their involvement in selecting staff and also because of their inspection role. This feeling of threat is usually lessened when adviser and teacher know each other well.

Advisory teachers

Advisory teachers can offer many of the things which advisers can offer, but have the advantage in the eyes of teachers of being close to the classroom and having no involvement in promotion or inspection.

Advice on classroom practice

Advisory teachers are selected for their skill as teachers and they should therefore be able to help other teachers in day-to-day classroom work.

Advice on materials, equipment and classroom organization

Advisory teachers, like advisers, should be able to offer information about the most recently published materials and the way they have been used in other schools.

Work with pupils in the classroom

An advisory teacher may work with a teacher in the classroom to try out new ways of working or introduce new ideas.

Lecture on classroom practice

Advisory teachers can usually offer stimulating talks about different aspects of teaching, based on first-hand experience either from their own work or from that of other teachers whom they have seen at work.

Problems in using advisory teachers

Advisory teachers, like advisers, are comparatively few on the ground and may therefore be pressed for time. There may also be a certain arbitrariness in the subject areas in which they operate in some LEAs, so that some subjects are well provided and other subjects not at all. There may be a certain protocol in inviting them into school. It may be necessary to go through the adviser or other officer to whom the advisory teacher is responsible.

Teachers from other schools

In a number of LEAs groups of teachers have been trained to offer in-service activities to other teachers. There may also be teachers in a neighbouring school who have developed particular work which is of interest.

Specific training in particular areas of work

The groups which have been trained to contribute will have planned courses in the areas of work where training is necessary and will be able to offer a school staff a complete programme or a contribution to their own programme.

Lectures on particular classroom work

A practising teacher who has developed some particular work is often a stimulating speaker.

Problems in using practising teachers

Practising teachers may have difficulty in finding sufficient time to offer in-service work to colleagues in other schools. Not all good teachers of children are good teachers of adults.

Local industry

Local industry may contribute to a school's professional development programme in several ways.

The provision of places on the firm's own courses

Some firms run courses which are highly relevant for teachers and may be prepared to offer one or two places to staff in a local school.

The provision of work experience for teachers

Work experience can provide an important developmental opportunity for teachers if it is carefully planned.

Information about the firm's staff development programme

Some firms have training programmes of high quality from which schools can learn. This would need to be discussed and investigated but a training officer might be able to offer useful advice to a school.

Problems in using local firms

Activities of this kind need to be carefully negotiated since not all firms have programmes which offer anything to schools and the firm has only a limited amount to gain from offering such opportunities to schools.

13

Evaluation

One of the major changes in in-service training is in the emphasis currently being placed upon evaluating what is happening. LEAs are now required to demonstrate that they are evaluating the programme they offer and it is equally important for schools to evaluate their own programme.

Evaluation is not something to be left to the end of a programme of professional development. An element of evaluation is required in the beginning in assessing needs. It is also required as a part of appraisal. Then there is value in formative evaluation while the course is running. Evaluation of the effects of any particular programme should be planned as the programme is planned and time and resources allowed for it.

Definitions

Buckinghamshire, quoted in a survey by Nebesnuick[87] defines evaluation as follows:

the process of conceiving, obtaining, analysing and communicating information and forming judgements for the guidance of educational decision-making with regard to specified aspects of education.

O'Sullivan, Jones and Reid[88] differentiate between monitoring, which they define as 'a short term, immediate check on the delivery of staff development activities' and evaluation which is 'a longer term judgment as to the worthwhileness of the staff development event or series of events'.

Oldroyd and Hall[27] note that there is a place for both formative and summative evaluation and for review which they suggest is a consideration of whether assumptions, aims, priorities and approach should be changed.

Planning evaluation

If evaluation is to be planned from the beginning of any professional development activity the professional development committee must be aware of the need to do this and prepared to allocate funds for the purpose. Responsibility for evaluation should be clearly delegated and care taken to see that there is access to expertise, either by ensuring that a member of staff is trained for the purpose or by buying in expertise either for evaluation or for training staff to undertake evaluation.

Michael Eraut[89] speaks of the need to allay suspicion and gain co-operation and support for evaluation. This is most likely to be achieved by openness and by considering the ownership of the evidence. The course participants need to know exactly what is being done by way of evaluation and the function of the evaluator. They are more likely to be co-operative if they have the opportunity to discuss the evidence and influence what goes into the final report. This does not mean that they decide what the evaluator says in the report, but that they hear about it before the report is written, rather as staff hear about the comment on HMI reports.

He also suggests a need to consider the possible consequences of evaluation which could be a change of programme, and the possible effect of evaluation on what actually happens as part of the course.

There are a number of questions which need to be considered in relation to evaluation. Oldroyd and Hall[27] suggest several issues which an evaluation brief might cover

1 the purpose and possible consequences of the evaluation
2 the audience for any summative report
3 the key questions
4 the methods of collecting evidence
5 the sources of the information
6 the time available and the deadline.

One further issue which should be covered is that of who should evaluate. Each of these points is developed in the paragraphs following.

The purpose and possible consequences of the evaluation

Easterby-Smith[90] suggests that evaluation has three main purposes: proving, improving and learning.

Proving

This aims 'to demonstrate conclusively that something has happened as a result of staff development and that this was worthwhile'.

Improving

This concerns current and future programmes and tries to ensure that they become better than they are at present.

Learning

This recognizes that 'evaluation cannot . . . be divorced from the process on which it concentrates and . . . this slight problem might well be turned to advantage by regarding evaluation as an integral part of the learning and development process itself'.

Accountability

A further important purpose is that of accountability. It is necessary to demonstrate that resources have been properly used and that the provision represents value for money. In the case of many courses it should be possible to demonstrate that there are changes in practice as a result. This may not be a fair expectation for courses which are aiming at broad long-term development, where results may not be evident for some time.

Perception

Jean Rudduck[48] also suggests that evaluation is a means of deepening participants' perception of the evaluation and what it can offer and that it may help them to understand and develop evaluation skills.

The audience for any summative report

Different audiences will have different interests and the report needs to be written with this in mind. The interests of the headteacher and staff of a school will be primarily concerned with whether the provision is resulting in improved practice in classrooms and elsewhere in the school. They will also share with the governors an interest in whether the school appears to be getting value for money in any provision made; the LEA will also be interested in this. The actual language used in the report may differ if it is to be a report only for the headteacher and senior staff from that used if it is to be a report only for the governors or a report intended for both.

The key questions

If evaluation is to be effective, it is essential that the course objectives are stated in a form which can be seen to be achieved. The following questions are common to many evaluations:

1 How far has the course achieved its stated aims?
2 Were the techniques and strategies chosen by the course tutor the most effective to achieve the course aims?
3 How far has the course met the needs and expectations of the course participants?
4 What evidence is there that the course has affected practice?
5 Has the course kept within the budget allocated?
6 What has been the cost of the course per participant?
7 Could the same results have been achieved more cheaply?

In any particular situation there will also be more specific questions which evaluation must try to answer. It is important to spend time and thought on identifying these questions so that the evaluation brief drawn up gives clear guidance about what those commissioning the evaluation wish to get from it.

The methods of collecting evidence

All evaluation depends upon sampling evidence of some kind. The evidence chosen and the size of the sample depend upon the purpose of the evaluation and the resources available. (Methods of evaluation are discussed in greater detail later in this chapter.) There are three basic ways of collecting evidence: from documentation, from observation and from people.

Documentation

This might include course descriptions; minutes of relevant meetings; course readings and teaching materials, notes for course tutors; reports by course members; notes by course members; course registers and records of attendance.

Observation

Observation might include notes of various kinds made during the time a course is taking place and might also include classroom observation after the course to see how far the experience had affected the work of the teachers concerned.

People

Evidence from people can be gathered directly in interviews or indirectly in questionnaires. Interviews can be in groups, where a specific agenda of issues can be discussed.

The sources of the information

Everyone concerned with the course will want to know how the evaluator is going to work and the sources he or she will use. This means that this is part of the information to be made clear at the beginning to everyone involved. Otherwise there will be considerable suspicion about what is happening.

The time available and the deadline

If evaluation takes too long it loses its value because the activity being evaluated will be largely forgotten. It is therefore important to have a clear timetable and a deadline by which the report will be ready.

Who should evaluate

Evaluation could be carried out either by someone from within the school or by an external evaluator. The decision about this is partly a matter of cost and partly a matter of where the appropriate skills and knowledge may be found.

Jean Rudduck suggests that an evaluator needs the following skills and qualities:

1 some research skills
2 knowledge of the education system
3 capacity to relate to people readily
4 skills of listening and observation
5 reliability in producing a report on time
6 credibility in the eyes of participants.

Many teachers will have some of these qualities and skills but only a limited number of teachers have research skills. If this kind of skill is not available it may be a good idea to buy in expertise in evaluation in the first place and then to build up expertise within the school. It should be remembered, however, that it is much more difficult for a teacher in the school to be objective; even when a school has developed its own expertise an external evaluator may be needed from time to time to provide a check. One possibility is that two schools could train members of staff in evaluation techniques and then evaluate each other's work occasionally.

Evaluation techniques

In planning evaluation it is important to use a variety of techniques which represent varying degrees of subjectivity and objectivity. Only a limited number of aspects of in-service training can be assessed objectively and subjective assessment must play an important part. Subjective assessment can be made more reliable by ensuring that a number of observations are made which complement and perhaps confirm each other.

There are a number of evaluation techniques which may be useful, which we shall discuss in more detail.

1 Questionnaires
2 Other documentary evidence
3 Discussion
4 Interviewing
5 Observations
6 Evidence from pupils
7 Value for money assessment.

Questionnaires

Questionnaires are a very common form of evaluation of in-service courses. Some can be completed quickly by the course members at the end of the course and others completed after a period. Some can be completely structured, with detailed questions which require ticked answers, perhaps grading the course under a series of items. The completely structured questionnaire has the advantage that the evaluator gets answers in a form which is easy to analyse and which covers all the aspects of the course which are of interest. On the other hand, there may be no opportunity for course participants to say anything about the issues which concern them, which may be important.

Alternatively course participants can be given a completely open statement which asks them to comment on any aspects of the course they wish. This certainly provides information about the concerns of the course members, but may not give the information which the evaluator is looking for and is much more difficult to analyse. It can be very valuable as material to discuss with a group of participants.

Other questionnaires provide a mixture of the two which would seem more likely to give a full picture. Leslie Ray[91] suggests a questionnaire which asks for feelings about the course, giving sentence completion tasks like:

The major feeling I have about this learning event is

. . . .

It can be valuable to give participants the same questionnaire again after a period to see if their views of the course have changed with time. It is also useful at this stage to ask questions about how far the course has affected practice.

Leslie Ray also suggests a course audit at the end of each day at a long course, asking questions like:

1 What have you learned today?
2 What helped the learning?
3 Was there anything that hindered your learning today?
4 If so, how did this happen?
5 Was there anything you would have liked to spend more time on/less time on/omitted?

The information gained is then discussed next day or when next the group meets. Ray also suggests at the beginning of the second and subsequent sessions asking people for three words which reflect their feelings about the previous session. These are put on a flip chart and discussed. He makes the point that it is important in a long course to evaluate as you go along, since important points about the beginning of the course may be forgotten by the time the end is reached.

Another way of tackling this is to have a large sheet of paper or small individual sheet available for comments to be made at any time. It may be difficult to get people to use these, however, when they are absorbed in the course.

Other documentary evidence

All the materials prepared for the course provide evidence for the evaluator. Documents other than questionnaires can be obtained from course tutors. Michael Eraut[89] suggests that representatives of the course members may help to collect evidence and that a working party of members might produce a report on the course or individual members produce their own reports. Course tutors might also be asked to produce a note of their reactions to the course.

Discussion

Discussion at the end of a course can be useful but needs careful structuring if it is to produce results. Simply asking for opinions produces some responses but these tend to be either positive or strongly felt negative comments. This is particularly likely to be the case if the course tutors are present.

Variations on nominal group technique are likely to produce useful results. Participants can be asked to work in pairs or trios and list, for example, six good things and six bad things about the course. They can then compare these with another pair and report on them to the whole group. In nominal group technique, the list of good and bad points is built up on a flip chart and there is a vote for the order in which they should be.

Another possible technique is to take points raised by participants in an open questionnaire and use these for discussion. They can be organized into a delphi questionnaire where course members are asked to grade how far they agree with each point. The points where there are differences of opinion are then discussed.

Interviewing

The evaluator can arrange to interview individuals and small groups. This can be a structured interview with everyone asked the same questions or a more open interview with the opportunity to pursue any question which seems to be of interest. As with the questionnaire, there would seem to be some advantage in an interview which is a mixture of the two.

A group interview can often be of value because people suggest ideas to others in what they say. On the other hand they may also influence others and the evaluator has to be aware of this.

There will also be a good deal of casual information in talking to people during the course.

The difficulty about interviewing as a form of evaluation is that it is very time-consuming. It is rather less so when group interviews are held and a sample group or so may be useful.

Observations

There are many opportunities for the evaluator to make observations of what is happening. The pre-course material can be studied and considered for its clarity of purpose and the extent to which it gives course participants a good idea of what they will experience. The teaching techniques employed by the course tutor can be noted and their success with the participants observed. The balance of the use of time in different activities can be measured and the extent of participant involvement will be evident from the way the participants respond.

In some courses it may be helpful to ask teachers to keep diaries of what is happening and these will be useful for evaluation if their owners are willing to share them.

After the course it will be important in many cases to know whether there is any difference in the way teachers are working. This will require observation, but it will also require some knowledge of how each particular teacher worked before the course.

Another possible way of making observations is to record all or part of what happens on audio or video tape. This has the disadvantage of being time-consuming to work through but can offer useful material for discussion with groups of course members.

Evidence from pupils

If a course is intended to change teachers' performance in the classroom, the most important evidence could come from pupils. As we saw earlier the problem about this is that not all teachers are prepared to ask direct questions of pupils about how they are doing and the task of the evaluator in getting at the information which the pupils have to give is one requiring considerable tact.

Obtaining information from pupils without upsetting teachers is largely a matter of finding suitable questions. For example a questionnaire listing different approaches to teaching and asking which of these has been used in the last term would probably be acceptable to teachers. This would make it possible to go on to ask whether there was any difference in the balance of the teaching approaches between the beginning and end of the term.

Information about what is happening in classrooms will also be obtained from looking at pupils' work and talking to them about it.

Value for money assessment

It is important to consider how much the course has cost per person and to weigh this costing against alternative ways of doing the same thing. Course costs should include fees and expenses of any external contributors, cost in staff time of arranging the course, any travel, accommodation, subsistence or other costs incurred by participants, cost of participants' time (or of supply teachers).

Selecting a technique

In selecting which of the techniques to use a school should have in mind the time involved both during the course and the time involved for evaluation as well as the cost in money. The amount of evaluation which can be done is limited but some should be done for every course. Courses which are expensive should be accorded a larger evaluation budget, so that value for money can be kept in mind.

The evaluation report

Evaluation should result in a report which is considered by the professional development committee, the headteacher and the governors. This will be a drawing together of all the evidence by the evaluator.

There are problems about this. Parlett and Hamilton[92] describe the problems as follows:

> Foremost is usually concern over the 'subjective' nature of the approach. Can 'personal interpretation' be scientific? Is not collection, analysis and reporting of data, skeptics ask, entirely at the discretion of the resear-

chers themselves? Behind such questions lies a basic but erroneous assumption that forms of research exist which are immune to prejudice, experimenter bias and human error. This is not so. Any research study requires skilled human judgments and is thus vulnerable. Even in evaluation studies that handle automatically processed numerical data, judgment is necessary at every stage, in the choice of samples, in the construction or selection of tests; in deciding the conditions of administration; in selecting the most suitable statistical treatment; in the relative weight given to different results, and particularly in the selection and presentation of reports.

One possible way round this problem is for the evaluator simply to give the data, leaving it for others to draw conclusions. If this is the approach wanted it should be made clear at the outset and time set aside for the necessary discussion. This approach will require the involvement in follow-up discussion of everyone involved in the course. If, on the other hand, the evaluator is expected to draw some conclusions from the evidence assembled, this too should be clear from the beginning but the discussion need not necessarily involve so many people or take so long.

The report should cover the ground which was set out in the brief. Where it is likely to be critical, it is wise to give those concerned some prior notice of what will be said.

Generally speaking the report should cover all aspects of the course with comment on the planning, the arrangements at the course venue, pre-course material, teaching methods and their effect on learning, handouts, the reactions of the participants, immediately and after an interval and any observed effects on practice.

Conclusion

This book has been written as if professional development were a linear process with everyone working through stage after stage. In practice it is more of a cyclic process with development going on all the time and different development activities interweaving with each other. In the linear pattern evaluation is the last stage of the development process. In the cyclic pattern it may well be the first stage of the next cycle.

The development of a teacher starts when he or she is a child in school observing the styles of the teachers there. It continues through initial training; in a school where development is taken seriously it will continue until retirement. There is always something new to learn in teaching. There may be new content and research is continually showing us new and better ways of enabling pupils to learn.

Any school which wishes to develop as an organization must enable all members of staff to develop in their work.

Appendix 1 Self-evaluation forms

Self-evaluation form 1

NAME...

DATE...

JOB DESCRIPTION

(Both appraiser and appraisee should have copies of the job description at the appraisal interview)

Is your present job description a true reflection of your present role and responsibilities? If not, please state areas of work which have altered in any way.

Are you satisfied with your present job description? If not, state any changes you would like.

THE YEAR'S WORK

What do you feel you have achieved this year?

Which aspects of your work have given you greatest satisfaction?

Which aspects of your work have given you least satisfaction?

PROBLEMS AND DIFFICULTIES
Were there any particular problems hindering your work in the last year?

PROFESSIONAL DEVELOPMENT
What opportunities have you taken for your own professional development during this year?

What other training needs do you feel you have?

GOALS
(Appraiser and appraisee should each have a copy of the previous year's goals at the interview.)
Which goals have you achieved?

Which goals have you not achieved or only partly achieved?

WORK PLAN FOR THE COMING YEAR
Please state your main goals for the coming year, how and when you plan to achieve them and how you will assess your success in achieving them

SIGNED...

Self-evaluation form 2

Please tick the appropriate box to indicate your self-appraisal under each heading.

How do I rate my	High	1	2	3	4	5
General teaching ability						
Knowledge of how pupils develop and learn						
Preparation and planning						
Presentation, questioning, leading discussion						
Classroom organization, including arrangements for group and individual work						
Success in meeting the needs of individuals						
Classroom management and control of pupils						
Development of pupils' initiative/independence						
Use of enviroment internal/external						
Record-keeping						
Use of appropriate resources						
Teaching of National Curriculum/use of schemes/guidelines						
Relationships with children						
Relationships with parents and others in the community						
Relationships/co-operation with colleagues						
Effectiveness in pastoral responsibilities						
Contribution to the life of the school						
Commitment to own professional development						

Self-evaluation form 3

Where a teacher is in a management role within the school, it will also be necessary to consider how well he or she is doing in relation to the check-list below.

Please tick the appropriate box to indicate your self-appraisal under each heading.

How do I rate my	High	1	2	3	4	5
Organization of work within my areas of responsibility						
Ability to lead colleagues, drawing together their ideas and developing good practice						
Ability to support, influence and develop the work of colleagues for whom I am responsible						
Work in liaising with colleagues in complementary roles in feeder and transfer schools						
Effectiveness in maintaining records for which I am responsible						
Effectiveness in reviewing and evaluating the work for which I am responsible						
Work in liaising with teachers in related areas of responsibility						
Consideration of recent reports and developments in the areas for which I am responsible						
Effectiveness in keeping others informed about the work in my areas of responsibility						
Skill in counselling colleagues who need my help						
Skill in running meetings						

Appendix 2   Classroom checklists

CLASSROOM CHECKLIST 1

SCHOOL...

TEACHER...

CLASS(ES) SEEN...

DURATION OF VISIT...

LESSON TOPIC(S)..

DATE..

POST..

....

INSPECTOR................................

....

PREPARATION AND PLANNING
(Objectives, clarity of planning, continuity, work on National Curriculum)

ORGANIZATION
(Beginning and end of lesson, changes of activity, differentiation, extent of independent work, grouping)

PUPILS' WORK
(Match of work to ability, ground covered, appearance, quality of marking)

TEACHER PERFORMANCE
(Appropriateness of teaching methods, provision for all abilities, good use of pupils' experience, skills in questioning, use of praise, pupil participation, clarity of instructions, discussion, management of pupils' difficulties, use of resources, control)

PUPILS' PEFORMANCE
(Extent to which pupils are on task, discussion skills, answering questions, concentration, work, independence)

TEACHER/PUPIL INTERACTION
(Relationship, the way the teacher speaks to pupils, teacher expectation, concern for equal opportunities)

PUPIL/PUPIL INTERACTION
(Behaviour of pupils to each other, the way they speak to each other, their readiness to help each other, the extent to which they work together)

ENVIRONMENT
(Overall attractiveness, layout for work, quality of display, safety)

**GENERAL
COMMENTS**

Signed _____

CLASSROOM CHECKLIST 2

SCHOOL..

TEACHER..

CLASS(ES) SEEN...

DURATION OF VISIT..

LESSON TOPIC(S)..

DATE...

POST...

....

INSPECTOR.................................

....

PREPARATION AND PLANNING

Teaching objectives clearly set
Planning takes account of continuity
Lesson clearly thought out
Clear relationship with National Curriculum

PUPILS' PERFORMANCE

Extent to which pupils are on task
Performance in discussion
Ability to answer questions
Concentration
Quality of group work
Degree of independence in learning

ORGANIZATION

Beginning and end of lesson
Organization for changes of activity
Provision for pupils of different abilities
Extent to which pupils work independently
Grouping of pupils
Control of pupils

TEACHER/PUPIL INTERACTION

Teacher/ pupil relationship
The way the teacher speaks to pupils
Teacher expectation of pupils
Evidence of concern for equal opportunities
                                    for race
                                    for gender
                                    for ability
                                    for social class

PUPILS' WORK

Match of work to pupils' ability
Ground covered in pupils' work
Appearance of work
Quality of marking

PUPIL/PUPIL INTERACTION

Behaviour of pupils towards each other
The way pupils speak to each other
The readiness of pupils to help each other
The ability of pupils to work together

TEACHER PERFORMANCE

Demonstrates a variety of teaching methods
Chooses appropriate strategies for the
whole ability range
Builds on earlier experiences , knowledge,
skills and concepts
Chooses appropriate questioning techniques
Uses praise and positive feedback
Encourages pupil participation
Gives instructions/explanations clearly
Leads discussion effectively
Chooses appropraite resources
Uses them effectively
Handles pupils' difficulties effectively
Exercises appropriate control

THE ENVIRONMENT

Overall attractiveness
Suitability of layout for work
Safety
Quality and appearance of display
Frequency of change of display

RATING SCALE

X	Demonstrates above-average skills
P	Meets performance standards required
I	Needs to improve
U	Unsatisfactory
N	Not observed or not applicable

Appendix 3 Appraisal record form

NAME ....

POST..

PERIOD REVIEWED ....TO ....

OVERALL PERFORMANCE
Teaching

Pastoral care (secondary schools)

Management (where appropriate)

Contribution to the school

ANY PROBLEMS OR DIFFICULTIES

PROFESSIONAL DEVELOPMENT AND CAREER PLANS

ANY COMMENT BY TEACHER

SIGNATURES

Appraisee ....Date............................

Appraiser ....Date ....

Headteacher...Date ....

RECORD OF GOALS

NAME..

POST...

PERIOD REVIEWED..TO...

References

1 J. Megarry (1980) 'Selected innovations in methods of teacher education', in E. Hoyle and J. Megarry (eds) *Professional Development of Teachers*, London: Kogan Page.
2 Education Reform Act (1988) London: HMSO.
3 J. Wilson (1988) *Appraising Teaching Quality*, London: Hodder & Stoughton.
4 J. Pearce (1986) *Standards and the LEA*, Windsor: NFER/Nelson.
5 V. Hall, H. Mackay and C. Morgan (1986) *Headteachers at Work*, Milton Keynes: Open University Press.
6 HMI (1977) *Ten Good Schools*, London: HMSO.
7 G. Williams (1982) *Staff Development in Education*, PAVIC Publications, Sheffield City Polytechnic.
8 J. Cawood and J. Gibbon (1981) *Educational Leadership: Staff Development*, Cape Town: Nasou Ltd.
9 R. W. Morant (1981) *In-Service Education within the School*, London: Unwin Education.
10 DES (1986) Circular 6/86, *Local Education Authority Training Grants Scheme: Financial Year 1987–88*, London: HMSO.
11 W. Taylor (1980) 'Professional development or personal development', in E. Hoyle and J. Megarry (eds) *Professional Development of Teachers*, London: Kogan Page.
12 P. Perry (1977) Keynote address to OECD/CERI, International Workshop on School-Focused Inset, West Palm Beach, Florida.
13 B. Joyce (1980) 'The ecology of professional development', in E. Hoyle and J. Megarry (eds) *Professional Development of Teachers*, London: Kogan Page.
14 Manpower Services Commission (1985), *Arrangements for the TUEI Related In-Service Training Scheme (England and Wales)*, London: Manpower Services Commission.
15 M. Eraut (1975) 'Strategies for promoting teacher development', a paper presented to the Third Standing Conference on Curriculum Studies, Norwich.

16 R. McCormick and M. James (1983) *Curriculum Evaluation in Schools*, London: Croom Helm.

17 M. Fullan (1982) *The Meaning of Educational Change*, Ontario: Oise Press.

18 D. Trethowan (1987) *Appraisal and Target Setting*, London: Harper Education Series.

19 F. W. Herzberg (1966) *Work and the Nature of Man*, New York: World Publishing.

20 B. Joyce and B. Showers (1980) 'Improving in-service training: the messages of research', *Educational Leadership* 37, 5: 379–85.

21 P. Honey and A. Mumford (1982) *Manual of Learning Styles*, Honey Publications.

22 J. Elliott (1981) *Forward*, in J. Nixon (ed.) *A Teacher's Guide to Action Research*, London: Grant McIntyre.

23 DES (1975) *A Language for Life*, Bullock Report, London: HMSO.

24 DES (1981) *Mathematics Counts*, Cockcroft Report, London: HMSO.

25 M. W. McLaughlin (1976), 'Implementation as mutual adaptation change in classroom organization' Teachers College Record, 77, 3: 339–51.

26 C. Day, P. Whitaker and D. Wren (1987) *Appraisal and Professional Development in Primary Schools*, Milton Keynes: Open University Press.

27 D. Oldroyd and V. Hall (1988) *Managing Professional Development and Inset*, Bristol: National Development Centre for School Management Training.

28 J. Dean (1987) *Managing the Primary School*, London: Croom Helm.

29 J. Dean (1985) *Managing the Secondary School*, London: Croom Helm.

30 Surrey Inspectorate (1984) *The Primary School Review*; *The Secondary School Review*, Surrey: Surrey Education Committee.

31 K. Baker and J. Sikova (1979) *The SITE Project Evaluation Report no. 3 (AW) Covering for Staff Release and Absence: A Secondary School Case Study*, SITE Project, School of Education Research Unit, University of Bristol.

32 C. Day (ed.) (1986) *Staff Development in the Secondary School: Management Perspectives*, London: Croom Helm.

33 E. Hoyle (ed.) (1980) 'Professional development of teachers', in *The World Yearbook of Education*, London: Kogan Page.

34 A. E. Wise *et al.* (1985) 'Teacher evaluation: a study of effective practices', *Elementary School Journal* 86, 1: 61–121.

35 G. Lyons (1980) *Teacher Careers and Career Perceptions*, Windsor: NFER.

36 C. Morgan, V. Hall and H. Mackay (1983) *The Selection of Secondary School Headteachers*, Post Report, Milton Keynes: Open University Press.

37 R. Bolam, K. Baker and A. MacMahon (1979) *The Teacher Induction Pilot Scheme*, final national evaluation report, School of Education, University of Bristol.

38 R. Tisher, J. Fyfield and S. Taylor (1978) *Beginning to Teach, Vol. 1: The Induction of Teachers: A Bibliography and Description of Activities in Australia and United Kingdom*, Report on stage 1 of the Teacher Induction Project ERDC Report no. 15, Australian Government Publishing Service.

39 DES (1983) *The Treatment and Assessment of Probationary Teachers*, administrative memorandum, London: DES.

40 *Guidelines for Review and Institutional Development (GRIDS)* (1983) London: Longman for the Schools Council.

41 L. Button (1982) *Group Tutoring for the Form Teacher*, Books 1, 2, London: Hodder & Stoughton.

42 E. Ballinger (1986) 'The training and development needs of managers: an overview',

in C. Day and R. Moore (eds) *Staff Development in the Secondary School*, London: Croom Helm.

43 B. Kerwood and S. Clements (1986) 'A strategy for School-based Staff Development', in C. Day and R. Moore (eds) *Staff Development in the Secondary School*, London: Croom Helm.

44 Manpower Services Commission (1987) *Summative Report on the Trist Scheme*, London: Manpower Services Commission (now the Training Agency).

45 J. Elliott-Kemp and G. Williams (1980) *The DION Handbook (Diagnosing Individual and Organisational Needs)*, PAVIC Publications, Sheffield City Polytechnic.

46 J. Elliott-Kemp and B. West (1987) *Sigma (Self-Initiated Group Managed Action)*, PAVIC Publications, Sheffield City Polytechnic.

47 P. Bamber and J. Nash (1989) 'Under the spotlight', *Times Educational Supplement*, 24 February.

48 J. Rudduck (1981) *Making the Most of the Short In-Service Course*, London: Methuen Educational for the Schools Council.

49 DES (1983) Circular 1/83, *Assessments and statements of special educational needs*, London: HMSO.

50 J. Dean (1984) *Teachers Learning*, Newcastle-upon-Tyne: Micro Electronics Education Programme.

51 R. W. Revans (1980) *Action Learning*, London: Blond & Briggs.

52 M. Pedlar (ed.) (1983) *Action Learning in Practice*, Aldershot: Gower.

53 K. Back and K. Back (1982) *Assertiveness at Work*, New York: McGraw-Hill.

54 S. Goulding (ed.) (1984) *Case Studies in Educational Management*, London: Harper & Row.

55 A. Paisey (1987) *School Management: A Case Approach*, London: Harper & Row.

56 Surrey Inspectorate (1975a) *Leading Discussion*, Media Resources Centre, Glyn House, Ewell, Surrey.

57 Surrey Inspectorate (1976) *Talking to a Group*, Media Resources Centre, Glyn House, Ewell, Surrey.

58 Surrey Inspectorate (1975b) *Interviewing*, Media Resources Centre, Glyn House, Ewell, Surrey.

59 M. Robson (ed.) (1984) *Quality Circles in Action*, Aldershot: Gower.

60 D. Francis and M. Woodcock (1982) *50 Activities for Self-Development*, Aldershot: Gower.

61 M. Woodcock (1979) *Team Development Manual*, Aldershot: Gower.

62 DES (1983) *Teaching Quality*, Cmnd 8836, London: HMSO.

63 Secretary of State for Education. Letter to Chief Education Officers, 10 December 1990.

64 Suffolk Education Department (1985) *Those Having Torches*, Suffolk County Council.

65 HMI (1985) *Quality in Schools: Evaluation and Appraisal*, London: HMSO.

66 National Steering Group (1988) *Report of the Consortium of School Teacher Appraisal Pilot Schemes*, Bristol: National Development Centre for School Management Training.

67 E. C. Wragg (1987) *Teacher Appraisal: A Practical Guide*, London: Macmillan.

68 P. Adams and D. Torrington (1989) 'Under the spotlight', *Times Educational Supplement*, 24 February.

69 R. Bollington and D. Hopkins (1988) *Teacher Appraisal for Professional Development: A Review of Research*, Cambridge Institute of Education.

70 G. Egan (1987) *The Skilled Helper*, Monterey, Calif., Brooks/Cole Publishing.

71 D. Montgomery (1984) *Evaluation and Enhancement of Teaching Performance*, Kingston Polytechnic, London.

72 Suffolk Education Department (1987a) *Teacher Appraisal: A Practical Guide, Part 3*, Suffolk County Council.

73 Suffolk Education Department (1987b) *In the Light of Torches*, London: Industrial Society.

74 DES (1986) *ACAS Report of the Appraisal and Training Working Group*, London: DES.

75 Somerset Education Committee (1988) *Review and Development – Progress Report, December 1986 – December 1987*, Taunton: Somerset Education Committee.

76 J. Elliott (1981) *Action Research: A Framework for Self-Evaluation in Schools*, TIQL Working Paper no. 1, mimeo, Cambridge Institute of Education.

77 T. Samph (1976) 'Observer effects in teacher verbal behaviour', *Journal of Educational Psychology* 68, 6: 736–41.

78 K. Lewin (1938) *The Conceptual Measurement of Psychological Forces*, Duke University Press.

79 K. F. Jackson (1975) *The Art of Solving Problems*, London: Heinemann.

80 C. Rogers (1961) *On Becoming a Person*, London: Constable.

81 F. Inskipp (1985) *A Manual for Trainers*, St Leonards-on-sea: Alexia Publications.

82 W. I. Stenning and R. Stenning (1984) 'The assessment of teachers' performance: some practical considerations', *School Organisation and Management Abstracts* 3: 77–9.

83 H. H. Meyer *et al.* (1965) 'Split roles in performance appraisal', *Harvard Business Review* 43, 1: 123–9.

84 D. Gill (1977) *Appraising Performance*, London: Institute of Personnel Management.

85 C. Donoughue, S. Ball, B. Glaister and G. Hand (1981) *In-Service: The Teacher and the School*, London: Kogan Page.

86 E. Hewton (1988) *School Focused Staff Development*, Lewes: Falmer Press.

87 D. Nebesnuick (1990) *Monitoring and Evaluation and the 1988 Educational Reform Act; Education Management Information Exchange (EMIE)*, Slough: National Foundation for Educational Research.

88 F. O'Sullivan, K. Jones and K. Reid (1988) *Staff Development in Secondary Schools*, London: Hodder & Stoughton.

89 M. Eraut (1985) *Evaluation of Management Courses*, Bristol: National Development Centre for School Management Training.

90 M. Easterby-Smith (1986) *Evaluation of Management Education, Training and Development*, Aldershot: Gower.

91 L. Ray (1986) *How to Measure Training Effectiveness*, Aldershot: Gower.

92 M. Parlett and D. Hamilton (1977) 'Evaluation as illumination', in M. Parlett and G. Dearden (eds) (1977) *Introduction to Illuminative Evaluation*, Calif.: Pacific Soundings Press.

Further reading

Abella, K. T. (1987) *Building Successful Training Programmes*, Wokingham: Addison-Wesley.

Baldwin, J. and Wells, H. (1979) *Active Tutorial Work*, Oxford: Basil Blackwell.

Ballinger, E. (1986) 'The training and development needs of managers: an overview', in C. Day and. R. Moore (eds) *Staff Development in the Secondary School*, London: Croom Helm.

Bolam, R. (ed.) (1982) *School-Focused In-Service Training*, London: Heinemann Educational.

Bolam, R. and Baker, K. (1981) *The Management of Staff*, Part 4, Block 6, Open University Course E 323, the Open University, Milton Keynes.

Dean, J. (1985) *Managing the Secondary School*, London: Croom Helm.

Dean, J. (1987) *Managing the Primary School*, London: Croom Helm.

Gough, B. and James, D. (1990) *Planning Professional Training Days*, Milton Keynes: Open University Press.

Hamblin, D. (1978) *The Teacher and Pastoral Care*, Oxford: Basil Blackwell.

Huczynski, A. (1983) *Encyclopaedia of Management Development Methods*, Aldershot: Gower.

Lyons, G. and Stenning, R. (1986) *Managing Staff in Schools: A Handbook*, London: Hutchinson.

Lyons, G., Stenning, R. and McQueeney, J. (1986) *Managing Staff in Schools: Training Materials*, London: Hutchinson.

Oldroyd, D., Smith, K. and Lee, J. (1984) *School Based Staff Development Activities*, London: Longman for the Schools Council.

O'Sullivan, F., Jones, K. and Reid, K. (1988) *Staff Development in the Secondary School*, London: Hodder & Stoughton.

Secondary Heads Association (1984) *The Appraisal of Teachers*, London.

Surrey Inspectorate (1975a) *Leading Discussion*, Media Resources Centre, Glyn House, Ewell, Surrey.

Surrey Inspectorate (1975b) *Interviewing*, Media Resources Centre, Glyn House, Ewell, Surrey.

Surrey Inspectorate (1976) *Talking to a Group*, Media Resources Centre, Glyn House, Ewell, Surrey.

Surrey Inspectorate (1986) *Negotiation*, Media Resources Centre, Glyn House, Ewell, Surrey.

Wallace, M. (1986) *A Directory of School Management Development Activities*, Bristol: National Development Centre for School Management Training.

Warwick, D. (1983) *Teacher Appraisal*, London: Industrial Society.

Wideen, M. F. (1987) 'Perspectives on staff development', in I. Andrews (ed.) *Staff Development for School Improvement*, Brighton: Falmer Press.

Winders, P. and Grieg, H. (1987) *Making the Best Use of Inset in Lancashire*, Preston: Lancashire Education Committee.

Index